London
of the
Future

The London Society

London of the Future

MERRELL
LONDON · NEW YORK

THE
LONDON
SOCIETY
EST. 1912

Contents

Foreword

Leanne Tritton

The first edition of *London of the Future* was published by The London Society in 1921. It is an eclectic and ambitious series of essays by professionals and civic leaders who were passionately concerned about the challenges of the time and how London might look in the future.

One hundred years later, in 2021, I was given one of the rare remaining copies to read after becoming chair of The London Society. I became one of the many thousands of Londoners who were able to be surprised and amused and to learn more about London from the work of these individuals.

Since the original book was published, the way in which we live has changed beyond even the wildest imaginings of the contributors. Fundamentally, though, the challenges we face remain unchanged. Health, transport, access to affordable and high-quality housing, and financial and racial inequality are still the issues of the day.

A century on, The London Society continues to be a place where Londoners can discuss, debate and shape the direction of the city. We are delighted to present the second edition of *London of the Future*, which we anticipate will provide much-needed provocation about the future of our wonderful city.

Readers and supporters who see this book at the time of its publication, in 2023, will need no introduction to the present context and lives of

Londoners. However, it is future generations whom I wish to address in this foreword.

In March 2020 London – along with the rest of the United Kingdom and much of the world – was placed in 'lockdown' owing to the COVID-19 virus. With limited exceptions, people across the globe were told to stay at home to stop the spread of the virus. Three years on, the unintended consequences on London are still to be fully realized, and predictions of how we will live, work and travel around the city vary depending on the motivations of the proposer.

In June 2016 the people of the United Kingdom voted in a referendum to leave the European Union, a decision that ushered in a period of political upheaval. Since the day of the vote, the country has had five prime ministers. The terms 'Brexiteer' and 'Remainer' have entered the dictionary, and identifying as either has become shorthand for categorizing an individual's attitude to almost any subject.

The world is just over twenty years into the introduction of search engines, and of those, Google is the most commonly used platform in the world, with 85 per cent of the market. Within those twenty years the social-media platforms Facebook (2004), Twitter (2006), Instagram (2010) and TikTok (2016) have been introduced, allowing anyone to share their thoughts on any subject, instantly, with little restriction. Imagine that. Political leaders around the world are still at the foothills of understanding how these platforms are affecting political and social debate, and how or if to regulate them.

Climate change is now recognized as a real threat to millions of people around the world, and rising temperatures are already changing the way in which we are able to inhabit the Earth. It is clear that we must change our way of living, and fast. But the ways of mitigating the impact of the damage and achieving 'net zero' have opened up another frontier of conflict as the monumental challenge to change every part of industry, food production and consumption will result in short-term winners and losers.

It is against this backdrop that you, the reader, can conclude that our political and civic leaders are dealing with all the issues of the past, with the added components of unrivalled speed of communication and a deadline for saving the way of life we currently enjoy. And something called AI has just started to become part of the vocabulary of the person on the street.

I hope that if you have received this publication in 2123, the ideas and thinking by our contributors have resulted in you living in a safe, prosperous, more equal and thriving London – and that you are a member of The London Society.

Old versus new, and indicators of the future.

Introduction

Peter Murray

The introduction to the first edition of *London of the Future*, published in 1921, was written by Sir Aston Webb, one of the leading architects of the day and now perhaps best known for having designed the principal façades of Buckingham Palace and the Victoria and Albert Museum. He was president of the Royal Institute of British Architects (1902–4), and chairman of The London Society, founded in 1912.

Sir Aston began his introduction by setting out the aims of the Society, many of which resonate with us today. He talked of influencing public opinion to impress the authorities with the importance of taking a wide view; of the preservation of all that is old and beautiful in London; and of the power of 'suggestion' – the promulgation of proposed improvements to the city.

In its early days, the Society was involved in suggestions for the treatment of the south side of the Thames, for improvements to Charing Cross and for London's road system. During the First World War, the Society organized teams of architects 'brought to distress through the war and unfit for military service' to draw up plans of London's major roads.[1] This *Development Plan of Greater London*, published in 1919, influenced thinking about shaping the city, ideas that can be found in Patrick Abercrombie's *Greater London Plan* of 1944. The Society's proposals were the first attempt to envisage the management of London as a functional metropolitan region and might be seen as the first *London Plan*.

The 1919 document pulled together many of the ideas for roads and open spaces being canvassed in the years before the First World War, but most importantly raised the idea of Greater London as an administrative whole. This was real future-thinking: while the Metropolitan Police had a broad area as its remit from its establishment in 1829, the concept of a wider metropolis was not given administrative force until the establishment of the Greater London Council in 1965, nearly half a century after the Society's proposals.

The idea of suggestion is a powerful theme that runs through the original *London of the Future*. In the book a wide variety of authors direct a critical eye to aspects of planning and development in London and posit suggestions for change. Some, like the Green Belt, have come to pass; others have not, such as the plans for small airships on Wormwood Scrubs, which were overtaken by aeroplane technology. Colonel R.C. Hellard – who had been director of the Ordnance Survey – wrote the chapter on roads, streets and traffic. He raised interesting points about the lack of wider town-planning and highlighted the fear that new housing schemes being developed in outer London could so encircle the capital that they might block every potential outlet for any new roads.

H.J. Leaning (also a contributor to an earlier treatise on building in London) revealed the Society's plans for 'welding our London railway systems into one consistent whole'.[2] More radically, he proposed getting rid of St Pancras, Cannon Street, Charing Cross, Fenchurch Street and Holborn Viaduct stations (the last of which was replaced in the 1990s by City Thameslink station), while converting Marylebone, London Bridge, Victoria and King's Cross to suburban or goods stations, with only Paddington, Euston, City (an amalgamation of Fenchurch Street and Liverpool Street stations) and Waterloo taking intercity trains. Leaning also wrote that the Post Office was experimenting with pneumatic tubes to distribute parcels, and called for this system to be extended across London with the capacity to move packages of up to 1 hundredweight (50.8 kilograms).

Some of the most radical – and in hindsight ridiculous – suggestions came from the politician Lord Montagu of Beaulieu, who advocated

Plate 1 of the *Greater London Plan* (1944) by Patrick Abercrombie and John Henry Forshaw shows districts defined by their function – 'University', 'Press' and so on – with blue dots for shopping streets and red for town halls.

airports over parks 'with, say, a winter garden underneath'. He looked to the day when aeroplanes would be able to alight on a much smaller space and householders could join together to provide a landing strip on the roofs of their homes.

Sir Arthur Fell MP wrote about a Channel Tunnel – of which he was an active promoter – that could carry 30,000 passengers and the same number of tonnes of freight over a 20-hour-long crossing between Britain and France (allowing 4 hours for repairs and change of staff). He also suggested a new bridge across the Thames – Temple Bridge – located between Waterloo and Blackfriars bridges, precisely the same spot for which the Garden Bridge was proposed nearly a century later.

The difficulty of crystal ball gazing is well illustrated by the chapter on the Port of London by the politician and businessman Hudson Kearley, 1st Viscount Devonport, who was then chairman of the Port of London Authority. Inspired by the idea of a British Empire on which the sun would never set, he foresaw continuous growth of the Port: 'the future of London as the greatest port of the Empire will be continuously assured'. Forty years later containerization proved the viscount wrong.

'Fortunately in London the tendency to decentralize has come in time', wrote the town planner, architect and engineer Raymond Unwin, as he set out thinking that was to affect attitudes to planning for the next fifty years. He thought that London as a single aggregation was too big. He foresaw growth of business and industry in the centre but suggested a finite size to the metropolis. He wrote: 'It is high time that a green belt was preserved around London to protect its inhabitants from disease, by providing fresh air, fresh fruit and vegetables, space for recreation and contact with and knowledge of nature.' The answer he put forward was satellite towns – a powerful idea that twenty years later made it into Abercrombie's *Greater London Plan* and was developed after the Second World War as the New Towns programme.

The idea of the Green Belt was picked up in greater detail by the architect David Barclay Niven in his chapter on parks and open spaces: 'It is necessary that there should be secured for all time an irregular belt of open space round London, including such splendid existing examples

The Thames beaches: a valuable, if unexpected, part of the city's 'green' spaces.

as Richmond Park, Banstead Downs, Epping Forest, Hampstead Heath and the nearer commons.' Niven recommended that this might be an average of about ¼ mile (400 metres) in width. He writes romantically of the simple freedom of meadows, of quiet ways, rustling woods and hospitable farms, as well as a 'circumferential boulevard' that would link together all the radial roads and provide a better distribution of traffic. These, too, are ideas that were consolidated by Abercrombie, although Niven probably did not imagine his boulevard would turn out like the M25 orbital motorway, or that the Green Belt would grow from 400 metres to 35 kilometres (22 miles) in width.

The final chapter of the 1921 *London of the Future*, by Robert Crewe-Milnes, 1st Marquess of Crewe, talks about the 'Spirit of London' – a survey of its streets and architecture, as well as literary characters that represent the great metropolis which, at that time, housed some seven to eight million souls. Lord Crewe suggests that in designing improvements to London, 'we cannot stand still, and we ought not to stand still, but we can advance with reverence and see to it that the immemorial spirit of London does not suffer amid the rush and stress of our modern life'.[3] This phrase encapsulates the aims of the Society since its foundation, and was reflected in its original Latin motto, *Antiqua tegenda, pulchra petenda, futura colenda*, which translates to 'Look after the old, seek the beautiful, cultivate the future'.

By the early twenty-first century the Society's activities had begun to focus increasingly on heritage and conservation, and as it moved into its hundredth year there was talk of closing it down. In 2013 a group of members decided to reinvigorate the charity, with a renewed focus on its original objects and the vision set out in *London of the Future*. The motto was changed to a more accessible 'Valuing the past; looking to the future', the membership began to grow again and, while maintaining its interest in London's history, the Society also concerned itself with positive change in the capital. So this new *London of the Future* brings together designers and thinkers to posit ideas for London as it develops over the next hundred years. While these do not necessarily represent the policies of the Society, they form a useful focus for future debate.

Although many of the ideas and suggestions set out in the original publication were made redundant by changing technology and attitudes, it is clear that the discussions generated by the Society promoted and reflected a direction of change that helped shape the capital in the twentieth century: the London of Abercrombie, of New Towns, orbital motorways, green belts and horror of density. This is in contrast to the more recent policies of the Urban Task Force that formed the basis of the *London Plan* at the start of this century: a London of denser development on brownfield sites located in areas with good public transport connections.

Today, as we face the radical changes to our way of life and the shape of the city brought about by COVID-19 and the climate emergency, the sort of radical thinking and imaginative suggestions made by the early members of the Society in *London of the Future* are particularly relevant, and I hope that the proposals in this book will have the power of their predecessors.

Notes

1   The London Society, *London of the Future* (E.P. Dutton & Co., 1921), pp. 18–19.

2   Ibid., p. 69. Leaning's earlier work: Horace Cubitt, H.J. Leaning and Sydney A. Smith, *A Treatise on the Law and Practice Affecting the Erection and Maintenance of Buildings in the Metropolis* (Constable, 1911).

3   *London of the Future*, p. 279.

One Embankment Place by Terry Farrell & Partners was constructed over Charing Cross station in 1990 and retrofitted in 2013 to high sustainability criteria.

The Art of Prophecy

Hugh Pearman

'Introductory Remarks on the Art of Prophecy' is the title of the disclaimer G.K. Chesterton inserts at the start of his vividly strange first novel, *The Napoleon of Notting Hill* (1904) – an imagined future of populist politics, civil unrest and rival warlords that begins, interestingly enough, in a London of 1984 and proceeds into the twenty-first century. Human beings play a game on futurologists, he says. 'The players listen very carefully and respectfully to all that the clever men have to say about what is to happen in the next generation. The players then wait until all the clever men are dead, and bury them nicely. They then go and do something else.'[1]

A warning to all us cleveristas. But he has a way around this problem. Amid a great deal of ponderous Edwardian satirical humour, Chesterton dismisses all the prophets of a future society, from the writer H.G. Wells to the noted Fabian Sidney Webb, and states that his London of eighty years hence will be 'almost exactly like what it is now'.[2] No science fiction or socialism for him: instead he envisages an alternative society to his own, a kind of parallel universe. One that has atrophied, grown tired of democracy and is ruled by an unelected king, a 'universal secretary'.

These are the colourless conditions in which his form of populist revolution breaks out. It starts with a learned man-child civil servant,

Auberon Quin, who by chance is made king, treats it as a huge joke and turns the London boroughs into independent fiefdoms with their own dashingly dressed militias. That is fine until a real revolutionary emerges, the Notting Hill Napoleon of the title, who takes all this flummery seriously enough to cause civil war.

Despite the novel's presentation as a light work, its message was taken seriously by some, allegedly including the young politician Michael Collins in his quest for Irish independence. The poet T.S. Eliot admired it. The London districts of the book are, of course, standing in for warring nations, an absurdist take on the inter-European tensions of the time. Today we might also see all this from the other end of the telescope: the fragmentation of previous blocs and political/economic alliances into ever smaller, inward-looking nativist entities.

For Chesterton's purposes, London as a city state, the centre of empire, was allegory enough: there is no sense of any nation beyond it, and only passing references to a world beyond that nation. Anyone attempting an equivalent novel today, with the United Kingdom's horizons so greatly reduced, would have even more reason to adopt this London-centric viewpoint.

While in Chesterton's day an enormous amount of power and wealth was concentrated in the manufacturing and trading cities of the Midlands and the North, with Liverpool at times exceeding London in income, the falling away of industry means that situation is utterly changed today: London has most of the money, as well as most of the power, in what is a highly centralized economy. What has not changed is the fear that stalked the Establishment then and does so now: that once things start to fall apart, chaos can ensue remarkably quickly. Chesterton, who liked to present himself as something of an anarchist in outlook, is enough of the Establishment himself to pull back a little. While celebrating the fictional chaos he unleashes on his version of London, he suggests finally that it is doomed to failure, glorious or inglorious.

In sketching out a possible future London, one has plenty of such reference material to draw on. Historians and economists tell us a lot, novelists and film-makers tell us more. Not about how things will be, just how they might be. After all, as Chesterton said, nobody knows. The irony is that he did better than most, prophecy-wise. His imagining of the impact of populist, identitarian politics turned out to be prescient for much of the twentieth century, and is especially so today. The rallying cry, the slogan, the impossible promise, is all that is needed to take,

The Royal Festival Hall is the only building to remain of the original structures for the Festival of Britain, held in 1951.

and in some cases keep, power. Realism is not attractive at a time of retrenchment.

To look forwards you have to look back, so I have to take into account the London of my own past. Being a child of the Home Counties, I had come to London at intervals to see the usual things – the museums, the Changing of the Guard, theatres and so forth. My family's assembly point for these excursions was usually the basement riverside restaurant in the Royal Festival Hall, handy for nearby Waterloo station. The most exciting thing in the vicinity for a small boy was the original narrow walkway across the Thames along one side of Hungerford Bridge, on a level with the trains rattling past only metres away. The London Society, in its book *London of the Future* in 1921, had called for the urgent demolition of this unlovely structure as a kind of negative war memorial: the glory of absence. Alas, it is still there today, but its iron girders are now part-concealed by two broader suspended walkways designed by Lifschutz Davidson and mounted either side.

Later I discovered the underused waterways of the capital. Even into the early 1970s these were semi-secret places, still industrial or post-industrial in character, with limited access. Once I walked the towpaths right across the capital from west to east, met almost nobody and saw remarkably few boats. This might well have been the start of the most persistent of my London imaginings, shared with many others: the capital deserted, even abandoned. Ever since then I've been fond of the experience of dereliction, something very different from the experience of destruction. Places just left unoccupied, untended, unwanted, forgotten, grown over. It's an indulgence. But the fortunes of cities rise and fall; this stuff happens.

When I started my first proper job in London towards the end of the 1970s, I got to know some of the statistics of the place, and one of the most telling was that London was still depopulating. There were plenty of new buildings and developments, of course, especially in the commercial sector, but there wasn't the population pressure, particularly on housing, that we are used to today. The Royal Docks were still working docks, but about to close. There were still some Second World War bombsites. Empty houses were much in evidence. Although 'gentrification' of streets of

The Thames Barrier, constructed in 1982 at Silvertown (north bank) and New Charlton (south bank), protects the floodplain of London from high tides and storm surges.

rundown terraces was well underway in such places as Islington, there was a lot more to do. When I bought my first flat in partially Georgian Clapton Square, Hackney, in 1980, the square was peppered with boarded-up windows and doors, and this was in no way remarkable. With few lenders, there was a 'mortgage famine' at the time and interest rates were offputtingly high. So this was not a roaring housing market, nor was there any prospect of one. Generally, squatting and protest occupations were commonplace, and helped to save a number of threatened parts of town, most notably Spitalfields.

The capital was still, obviously, the capital – there was no likelihood of it ceasing to exist in the way that we are told happened after the departure of the Romans in the early fifth century, when it supposedly became a ghost town, pillaged for its materials. It was deemed valuable enough to justify the cost of building the Thames Barrier, which I saw under construction as I went to and from work in Woolwich, and which came into operation in 1982. The eastern side of the country was very gradually tilting downwards, we were told, and this, combined with the storm surges that had caused devastating floods in the past, made the barrier essential. Despite the fact that its designers' planning analyses were made in 1970, gradually rising sea levels were taken into account.

It is now estimated that the barrier, which is deployed with increasing frequency, should continue to work well decades past its alarmingly early originally predicted obsolescence date of 2030. But this still allows plenty of time for the premise of another book about a future London to come to pass. Will Self's *The Book of Dave* (2006), set 500 years ahead, supposes an almost wholly flooded city in which only certain areas of high ground, such as Hampstead, survive as islands, and where an authoritarian religion has taken root, based on the rediscovered writings of a deranged London taxi driver. Self always defers to J.G. Ballard, in particular his 1962 novel *The Drowned World*, based on the premise of London becoming a lagoon following catastrophic global climate heating.

So London's population was still falling when the Thames Barrier was built. From its overall peak of 8.6 million as a whole in 1939, it fell steadily to some 6.8 million by the start of the 1990s. In inner London this trend was even more pronounced, with the population halving in number over fifty years. Despite accelerating growth from the 1990s onwards, the inner London boroughs are still in late 2022 a million short of the numbers they had hit during their earlier peak in 1931.[3]

Part of the reason for this was policy of course – slum clearance, people being encouraged to move to 'overspill estates' outside the capital, expanded satellite towns, the making of Milton Keynes and so forth. But in the late 1970s to early 1980s you couldn't help wondering occasionally what would happen to London as all this was happening. Terrorist bombs were going off, industries were closing, there were frequent power cuts, riots took place and – this being still the Cold War – we feared the ultimate Bomb.

A new plague was another cheerful possibility occasionally raised. Later, the deserted London of Danny Boyle's 2002 film *28 Days Later* inevitably came to mind during the first lockdown of the COVID-19 pandemic in 2020, when everyone was confined to their home, venturing outdoors was restricted, and the streets were so empty that in the residential areas of my bit of London you could walk easily in the middle of the roads. This was given added piquancy by the fact that Simon Pegg and Edgar Wright's 2004 spoof zombie-apocalypse horror movie *Shaun of the Dead* had been filmed in several of these same streets. I had seen those thespian zombies in the (convincingly rotting) flesh.

Scary movies and entertainingly speculative books aside, the notion of a catastrophe or combination of catastrophes making London either uninhabitable or very undesirable does not seem especially far-fetched, especially with a European war, involving a nuclear-armed aggressor, raging at the time of writing. Nor, given all those past years when the population of London was in steady decline, does a less traumatic return to depopulation seem impossible.

But let's assume that the present pressures on the capital continue more or less on the trajectory they have followed for the past several years, doubtless with some relaxation during periods of economic recession. The gradualist approach to urban renewal, all those bricky 'London Vernacular' housing blocks and new super-relaxed workplaces with wellness centres and cafés on roof terraces, go only so far. The bristling towers of investment apartments won't help at all until there is a sufficiently sharp property price crash for them to become affordable to people on normal incomes who might actually live there. And how many student flats can any city take? Meanwhile, if history has taught us anything, it is that the private sector can never be expected or trusted to provide enough social housing, no matter how many carrots and sticks and 'planning gain' clauses are applied. To do that you need a massively expanded state-funded programme of building social rented housing. Unfortunately, this is not permissible with currently prevailing ideologies.

I don't know what will happen, or how thin everything can be stretched before it breaks. Chesterton's warning against prophecy is ringing in my ears. But it partly depends on where you think London begins and ends anyway, and that brings in the railways. Never mind the extremities of the Elizabeth line and Thameslink, or those post-war new and satellite towns that were meant to provide the growth otherwise constrained in London by the Green Belt. We all know people who commute in from much further away. If I were that way inclined, I'd look to Derby or Nottingham. Homes are cheap there by London standards, and if work calls you into the office in London a day or two a week, the journey on the fastest trains takes about an hour and a half.

However, I am not that way inclined because another warning is ringing in my ears. My father was not one to hand out many pieces of life-advice to his sons but he did have two that I remember. One was 'It's best to steer clear of spirits' – he was the son of a wine and spirit merchant, knew the customers, and hardly ever touched the stuff. The other was 'never commute', said with feeling as a lifelong commuter on packed trains to his job at Post Office Telecoms headquarters in the City. I took his advice with regard to the latter and am fairly abstemious with regard to the single malts. So: we want to live, work and enjoy ourselves in *real* London, do we not? Not in London-in-the-Midlands, London-in-the-West-Country, London-by-the-sea?

For the sake of the rest of England rather than for Londoners, I would urge everyone not to abandon the Green Belt and return to 'England and the Octopus', as the committed ruralist Sir Clough Williams-Ellis described the unchecked ribbon-development sprawl of the 1920s.[4] But we can make the Green Belt *different*.

I am ever so tempted by the most radical proposal of them all, the joyful megalomania of the architect Peter Barber's 'Hundred Mile City' plan of 2017 for London accommodating 40 million people very congenially ('Build a street-based, linear city a hundred miles [160 kilometres] long, 200 metres [656 feet] wide and 4 storeys high. Wrap it round London').[5] But we know Barber is flying a kite in that particularly beguiling self-generated project, not because of its extraordinary level of ambition but because he gives us a great big clue: it contains a monorail, whizzing around the whole 100 miles.

Ha-ha, no. Monorails are the acknowledged signifiers of utopian projects that (being utopian) will never happen. The future London will not contain a monorail system, even though the past contains an everyday one that has been running happily in Wuppertal, Germany, since 1901. There's a reason why they didn't catch on. Ordinary railways are easier and better. Put them on elevated viaducts, like the Docklands Light Railway, when necessary, or underground on the cut-and-cover principle as part of the building programme, as used in the construction of the Metropolitan and District lines.

But that's just a detail, a bit of nostalgia for earlier imagined futures. The thinking that resulted in the Hundred Mile City is entirely serious and thoroughly sound. How do you massively densify London without it sprawling ever further outwards? And to those who claim that endless sprawl doesn't matter in the slightest, please take the delayed train service home. The human psyche needs the escape to something resembling nature, and everybody seems to have forgotten that we need farmland to grow food, and woodland to manage water and air quality and because we like it. The quickest way to lose useful and amenity countryside is to build at the car-dependent suburban densities we see spreading like mould around every market town in the United Kingdom.

So Barber's take on the accepted principle of densifying the suburbs makes sense as a polemic – particularly the bit where he talks about his wall-city expanding *inwards* rather than outwards, colonizing and urbanizing the

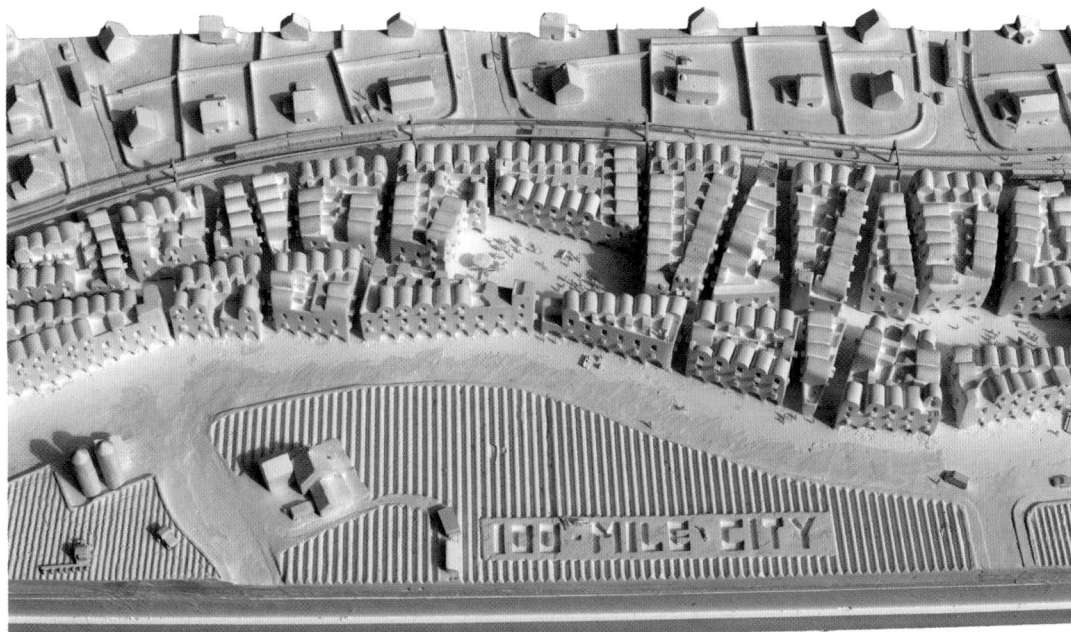

The Hundred Mile City by Peter Barber Architects: 'In time, watch our city grow inwards, spreading like a wildfire through wasteful, anti-social, car-choked suburbia.'

suburbs. The idea of it including a circular public transport system, linking the ragged ends of all the radial routes out of the centre, is plain obvious once you remove the word 'monorail'. His own buildings to date can be seen as erratic, displaced fragments of the Hundred Mile City.

That is, however, just too much building to be entertained right now, even in phases. The British fear and shy away from grand plans, especially if they live in a place where one is mooted. But one can imagine a London girt by something related, achieving its aims more stealthily. Something including a lot of places to live and work and play in, absorbing millions of people. Something that works with the natural world. Something that could ally with the rewilding movement (though don't forget the need to grow food). Well, as many have pointed out, we can start with the golf courses dotting London's periphery, can't we? What greater waste of space and of natural resources can there be than a shorn, irrigated golf course? On the 'greatest good for the greatest number' principle their score is risibly low.

But that's just a start. In a Chestertonian parallel urban universe, the post-war planning regime took a different direction, and has the edge of London defined by inhabited forests and clearings, home to a happy breed of Woodlanders, threaded through by tramways and providing everything anyone could need. This world is that of the urban planner Ebenezer Howard crossed with that of Peter Barber, with a hat-tip to the London National Park City Foundation.[6] This scenario also includes some of the thinking that informed the 'Oxford–Cambridge Arc' along the line of a restored railway linking those cities via Milton Keynes: a government-approved transport project (East West Rail) that is actually happening in fits and starts, even though the final section, an all-new track from Bedford to Cambridge, is some years off and vulnerable to short-termist spending cuts. A National Infrastructure Commission ideas competition for an Arc masterplan was won in 2017 by the 'VeloCity' consortium of consultants, and was notable for the way in which every new settlement was not only linked to public transport and to cycling and walking routes, but also included an area of common land for everyone to use.[7]

Everything has gone rather quiet on that (voters in the shires, *quelle surprise*) but luckily all these ideas are already implemented in my alternative-universe Woodlanders' edge-city to London, which, though I do say so myself, has proved to be remarkably successful over the years as it has matured and is now an example to the world. In this fiction, it exists. Perhaps, with all these good and workable ideas floating around, it might be considered in reality.

Notes

1 G.K. Chesterton, *The Napoleon of Notting Hill*, available at www.gutenberg.org.

2 Ibid.

3 See 'Population Changes over the Decades', Trust for London, www.trustforlondon.org.uk/data/population-over-time, accessed April 2023.

4 Clough Williams-Ellis, *England and the Octopus* (Geoffrey Bles, 1928).

5 See www.peterbarberarchitects.com/hundred-mile-city-1.

6 See www.nationalparkcity.london/national-park-city-foundation.

7 See www.tibbalds.co.uk/work/projects/velocity.

Borough Market: an old amenity brought to new life through increased concern for and awareness of the quality and provenance of fresh food.

Future Food City

Carolyn Steel

The supply of food to a great city is among the most remarkable of social phenomena – full of instruction on all sides.
GEORGE DODD[1]

What is the future of London's food, or rather, what can looking at London through the lens of food tell us about its future? Future-gazing is always fraught with uncertainty, yet of two things we can be certain: if London still exists one hundred years from now, its citizens will still need to eat; and unless food by that time is being made entirely in labs, at least some of London's sustenance will come from territories well beyond the city itself – the rural hinterland without which no metropolis can survive.

This would be nothing new: since its foundation in AD 43, London has imported much of its food. Established by the Romans at a natural ford across the River Thames, Londinium was soon a bustling port described by the historian Tacitus as a place 'frequented by a number of merchants and trading vessels'.[2] Much of that trade consisted of imports of olive oil, wine, pine nuts, raisins, pepper, ginger, cinnamon and *garum* (a fermented fish sauce), shipped in to keep the custodians of this chilly imperial outpost happy.[3] Such unusual goods would in many ways come to define London and, by extension, the nation of which it would one day become capital.

The constancy of London's food culture is in many ways a quality of the food itself. A Roman or medieval Londoner eating their daily meal would recognize much about a modern citizen doing the same. Twenty-first-century Londoners might subsist on ready meals or conjure up a late-night curry from an online food-delivery service, yet the act of eating itself – and all that it implies – remains largely unchanged. Like all great cities, London has always relied on its markets, takeaways, bars and taverns, and the daily thrum of Londoners producing, transporting, buying, selling, cooking and eating breakfast, lunch and dinner (with the odd snack in between) has provided the city's eternal heartbeat. London is a city shaped by food, which is why, as we attempt to peer into its food future, it makes sense to begin with its past.

London's history is inextricably bound up with its river, the conduit through which much of its food and wealth have flowed. By the year 1000, the port of Billingsgate was already busy trading with the Low Countries and Rhineland, while its rival Queenhithe served the Thames Valley, becoming the city's first grain market by the early thirteenth century. As a staple food of cities, grain was of paramount importance in the pre-industrial world, and its supply to medieval London was crucial for the city's wealth and that of its region. Market towns with access to the Thames, such as Faversham and Rochester in Kent, Henley in Oxfordshire, and Rye in Sussex, flourished, and by 1300 the London grain trade dominated the economy of southeastern England.[4]

London's appetite shaped the countryside, and food flowing in from the country shaped the city in turn. The medieval capital was bisected by a broad street running east from Newgate to Aldgate, whose names – Cheapside, Poultry and Cornhill – reveal it to have been London's main food market ('cheap' comes from the Old English *ceap*, 'to barter'). Another main road ran up from London Bridge and Borough Market (by the original Roman ford) to a major crossroads at Cornhill, near to which stood Leadenhall Market, on the site of the old Roman forum.

Like all pre-industrial cities, London was surrounded by market gardens, whose growers took valuable deliveries of 'night soil' (human and animal manure) in exchange for fresh fruit and vegetables, to be sold at markets including that at Covent Garden. Queenhithe and Billingsgate were respectively the city's chief grain and fish markets, the latter remaining on

Seventeenth-century London's foodways: John Ogilby's 'Large and Accurate Map of London' (1676), annotated with the old London markets. These were traditionally held at points where main streets came in from the surrounding areas.

its historic site until as late as 1984. London's sheep and cattle, meanwhile, were reared mostly on the rich grasslands of Scotland, Wales and Yorkshire, so approached the city from the northwest, streaming down then broad country lanes, such as St John's Street, to a 'smooth field' outside Newgate – this was Smithfield, London's meat and cattle market for more than 1,000 years.

Smithfield was the most visible, visceral manifestation of what it took to feed the pre-industrial metropolis: in its heyday, up to 30,000 beasts would gather there on the 'Great Day' before Christmas.[5] Smithfield was also central to London's conviviality, crammed with taverns fitted with huge public ovens, where people went either to socialize or to get a roasted bird or joint of meat to take away (few pre-industrial city dwellers had the means to cook at home). Such establishments formed the backbone of London social life until the 1650s, when coffee shops began to vie with them for supremacy: places where, for the price of a penny dish of coffee, customers could sit all day chatting to whoever might care to join them. Coffee shops soon became the places to go to find out all the latest news and gossip, and several newspapers were founded in them, as was the insurance market Lloyd's of London, whose agents once gathered in an eponymous coffee shop to get all the latest shipping news.

By the eighteenth century, however, London's most significant import was sugar, a luxury food obtained through the notorious 'triangular trade' that exchanged goods for enslaved people in West Africa, who were transported to the Caribbean and forced to turn sugar cane into what was described by Europeans as 'white gold'.[6] Although this trade operated out of such ports as Bristol and Liverpool, Londoners consumed the bulk of the sugar produced, creating a craving that blurred the distinction between the need and desire for food, and effectively gave birth to consumer society. In 1720 the writer Daniel Defoe noted the nation's general dependence on this new trade:

> It is not the kingdom which makes London rich, but London makes the rest of the kingdom rich ... The country send up their corn, their malt, their cattle, their fowls, their coals, their fish, all to London, and London sends back spice, sugar, wine, drugs, cotton, linen, tobacco, and all foreign necessaries to the country ... London consumes all, circulates all, exports all, and at last pays for all; and this is trade.[7]

By this time London's status as a global trading capital was assured. The city's favourable geography and status as capital of a buccaneering nation unafraid to use its military might to seize wealth from distant lands ensured its dominance. London's 'free trade' attitude was noted approvingly by the economist and philosopher Adam Smith in his *Inquiry into the Nature and Causes of the Wealth of Nations* (1776), in contrast to the city's landlocked rival Paris, whose lack of a navigable river rendered it incapable of competing on the global stage.[8] Smith agreed with Defoe that the 'great commerce of every civilized society is that carried on between the inhabitants of the town and those of the country', and that the 'gains of both are mutual and reciprocal'.[9] He went on to warn, however, that the 'inhabitants of a city ... situated near either the sea-coast or the banks of a navigable river ... may ... grow up to great wealth and splendour, while not only the country in its neighbourhood, but [also] all those to which it traded, were in poverty and wretchedness'.[10]

By the early 1800s such wretchedness was all too evident. Riding around rural southeastern England in a barely controlled rage, the writer and politician William Cobbett penned a series of diatribes lambasting the overblown city, which he dubbed 'the Wen' (a malignant boil), whose greed sucked all the wealth and goodness out of the surrounding countryside.[11] This was not, in fact, the first time that London's overweening power had attracted opprobrium. Back in 1516 the statesman and humanist Thomas More had criticized the city in his *Utopia*, an imaginary account of a far-off island of semi-independent city states where urban–rural harmony reigned and everybody farmed. By treating his account as fantasy, More just about got away with his polemic, but his implied criticism of King Henry VIII's bloated capital was clear.

By Cobbett's day, two centuries of enforced land enclosures had left much of the British countryside in destitution. This situation was only exacerbated by the arrival of railways and the repeal in 1846 of the Corn Laws (the removal of tariffs and restrictions on cheaper imported grain). Although industrialization was not the cause of urban–rural imbalance, the railway age nevertheless marked a turning point for urban life. The ability to transport food rapidly over great distances emancipated cities from geography, unleashing an explosion of urban development matched

Chicago Union Stockways, a hand-coloured postcard produced by Curt Teich & Co. and a stark illustration of the 'invention' of cheap meat.

by rural transformation. The effects were felt most keenly in the American Midwest, where railways opened up swathes of previously inaccessible grassland to grain production. When Chicagoan ranchers had the bright idea of feeding their surplus grain to cows, modern 'factory farming' was born, along with the 'cheap' meat that a moment's reflection ought to tell us shouldn't exist. As mountains of commodified meat and grain began to pour into unprotected European markets, including that of London, the global food system we know today took shape, together with a widespread rural depression from which many nations would never recover.

Horrified by the sight of impoverished farmworkers pouring into London's slums, the urban planner Ebenezer Howard came up with his famous proposal to revitalize the rural economy: the establishment of a network of semi-independent city states called garden cities.[12] Limited in size and surrounded by 'green belts' of dedicated farmland, garden cities were effectively More's *Utopia* replayed for the railway age. In 1903, with the backing of major industrialists including Joseph Rowntree, George Cadbury and the Lever brothers, work began on a prototypical garden city in Letchworth, Hertfordshire. Although Howard's plans for land reform failed to materialize, Letchworth did bequeath the capital one major legacy: the *Greater London Plan* of 1944 included a Green Belt 6 miles (10 kilometres) wide, designed explicitly to curb the city's future growth.[13]

Today the ideas behind the garden city are more relevant than ever. In an era of social and ecological crisis, in which many of the threats we face are either wholly or partly 'externalities' of the purportedly cheap, yet in reality ruinously expensive, industrially produced food upon which we rely, the need to review how and what we eat – and therefore how we live – could hardly be more urgent. In this respect, London's long history as a free-trade pioneer makes it the ideal starting point for reimagining the city, since it represents how we got here and, for that very reason, has inspired a plethora of alternative ideas.

Returning to our original question, therefore, what might London's food culture look like a hundred years from now? Since the feeding of cities is largely a question of geography (and the socio-economic conditions that spring from it), many of the answers arguably lie in the past, since today, after two centuries of effectively ignoring geography, we are once again entering an age in which few things will matter more.

As history demonstrates, London is in fact well placed to get far more of its food from its local region. Thanks partly to its protected Green Belt, the capital is still surrounded by the fields that fed the medieval city, and although modern London is far larger than its medieval counterpart, its historic market gardens in the Home Counties remain largely intact; they just grow commodity crops, such as cattle feed, rather than the apples and hops of old. The barriers to London eating more locally aren't primarily geographical, therefore, but rather socio-economic – which is to say that they could change.

What might bring about such change? In the eighteenth century Adam Smith assumed that the global free trade carried out by London in his day could generate unlimited wealth, on the basis that nature was infinite and came for free. Those assumptions no longer hold; instead, we belong to a neo-geographical age in which we must measure the ecological impact of everything we do. As far as food goes, a return to a more regional, seasonal, organic system makes compelling sense.

It's not hard to conceive of how such a shift might affect London, since it has already been imagined by virtually every utopian critic of the city. In his tract *News from Nowhere* (1890), for example, the designer, writer and activist William Morris told of a time traveller who wakes up in a London transformed by social revolution, in which roads have returned to 'pleasant lanes', culverts are restored to 'bubbling brooks' and Trafalgar Square is a sloping orchard full of apricot trees.[14] Freed from the shackles of capitalism, Londoners work mostly in agriculture or handicrafts, their faces 'frankly and openly joyous'.[15]

While Morris's dream is clearly fantasy, elements of it nevertheless resonate. Today, dwindling global resources mean that the rampant capitalism that shaped London has finally run its course, raising profound questions about the city's future. As the response to the COVID-19 pandemic demonstrated, many people are ready for a new way of life, one that allows them more time to spend with family and friends, pursuing hobbies or just being close to nature. Food could have a powerful role in shaping such an existence, since it remains what binds us most closely to one another and to the natural world. To value food again and put it back at the core of our lives is arguably our most direct route to living in balance with nature and thriving in a low-carbon future.

As utopians have long recognized, such a way of life necessarily involves bringing city and country closer together. Indeed, despite London's imperial past, much of its food was produced in the United Kingdom until quite recently. Before the Second World War, for example, special trains carrying broccoli and milk would come up from the southwest, and those carrying rabbits from the north, while the East End would empty out every September as some 40,000 Londoners left the city for their annual working holiday picking hops in Kent.

While a return to such an annual exodus seems unlikely, city dwellers are once more discovering the pleasures of working on farms, as the resurgence of interest in allotments and community gardens attests. Many Londoners yearn for closer contact with nature, and the social and health benefits of such activities are clear.[16] The sense of seasonality returning to the city would be another clear gain from such a revival. In our disembodied, digitalized world, food reminds us that life doesn't just exist in a numbing 24/7 vacuum of convenience, but is ultimately bound to the Earth and to planetary rhythms. A return to a more regional, humanized food system would also have the benefit of reviving London's food markets, and by extension the conviviality that once flourished there, counterbalancing the echo chambers of our screen-bound lives.

Such a food-based revival would arguably present London with its best opportunity to transform itself from a leading capitalist city into an exemplary ecological and socially just one. By valuing food and farmers, restoring local and regional markets, and conducting its global trade fairly and transparently (even Howard didn't imagine his garden citizens would give up coffee), the capital could become a beacon of urban renewal for the neo-geographical age. One of London's greatest legacies from its imperial past is that it is a mixed city: many of its most vibrant neighbourhoods and markets belong to its immigrant communities, whether they be Jewish, Chinese, Bangladeshi or Turkish, for example. By celebrating such food cultures and supporting and making space for their way of life, the city could express a new chapter in its global situation and make some reparation for its colonial past.

A more dystopian vision of London's food future (also presaged in its past) is one in which today's dominant socio-economic forces prevail: which is to say, the drive towards ever 'cheaper' food, at whatever cost, continues. Given that industrial farming is now humanity's most destructive activity, a transformation of the way in which we farm is inevitable over the next century. What shape this takes is the question. In the absence of a powerful alternative vision, the likelihood is that the current trend towards ever more highly processed industrial food will continue, controlled by an increasingly concentrated and unaccountable

Sitopia Farm in Greenwich: a vision of London's food future?

global food system. The effect on London could be dolorous: a city with a lifeless, branded public realm devoid of independent shops and cafés, surrounded by factory-like vertical farms and protein labs, whose citizens huddle indoors, subsisting on tasteless, faceless lab food delivered by drones owned by such tech giants as Amazon and Google.

A smorgasbord of potential food futures awaits London, from a Morrisian resurgence as an inclusive, convivial city of markets and local shops surrounded by regenerative orchards and farms, to an atomized, polluted dystopia devoid of character and joy – or something in between. Will London embrace the chance to renew and redeem itself through the healing power of food? Only time will tell – but as long as people eat, value and take pleasure in food, the potential will always be there.

Notes

1 George Dodd, *The Food of London* (Longman Brown, Green & Longmans, 1856), p. 1.

2 Tacitus, *The Annals*, Book XIV, chapter 33 (AD 59–62), in *Complete Works of Tacitus*, ed. Alfred John Church and William Jackson Brodribb (Random House, 1942).

3 See Richard Tames, *Feeding London: A Taste of History* (Historical Publications Ltd, 2003), p. 12.

4 In 1350 the estimated cost of carrying ¼ ton of wheat 10 miles (16 kilometres) was 3.5 pence by road, 0.3 pence by river and 0.2 pence by sea, so coastal ports such as Sandwich and Yarmouth could still afford to supply the city with grain. See B.M.S. Campbell et al., *A Medieval Capital and its Grain Supply*, Historical Geography Research Series, no. 30, 1993.

5 George Dodd describes the scene: 'On that day, 30,000 of the finest animals in the world were concentrated within an area of four or five acres. They had been pouring in from ten o'clock on the Sunday evening, insomuch that by daylight on the Monday they presented one dense animated mass, an agitated sea of brute life. All around the market, the animals encroached on space rightfully belonging to shop-keeping traffic; Giltspur Street, Duke Street, Long Lane, St John's Street, King Street, Hosier Lane – all were invaded; for the cauldron of steaming animalism overflowed from very fullness.' Dodd, *Food of London*, p. 244.

6 For a definitive account of the sugar trade and its effects, see Sidney Mintz, *Sweetness and Power* (Penguin, 1986).

7 Daniel Defoe, *Complete Tradesman*, II, chapter 6, quoted in Dodd, *Food of London*, pp. 110–11.

8 As London gorged on foreign foods and goods, Paris struggled to feed itself. This contrast would in many ways shape European politics, creating the British sense of exceptionalism that would eventually lead to the act of national self-harm that was Brexit.

9 Adam Smith, *An Inquiry into the Nature and Causes of the Wealth of Nations*, 2 vols., ed. Edwin Cannan (Methuen, 1925), vol. I, p. 355.

10 Ibid., p. 377.

11 'Have I not, for twenty years, been regretting the existence of these unnatural embossments; these white-swellings, these odious wens, produced by Corruption and engendering crime and misery and slavery? ... But, what is to be the fate of the greatest wen of all? The monster, called, by the silly coxcombs of the press, "the metropolis of the empire"?'; William Cobbett, *Rural Rides*, 2 vols (Reeves & Turner, 1885), vol. I, p. 52.

12 Ebenezer Howard, *Garden Cities of To-Morrow* (MIT Press, 1965).

13 See Robert Beevers, *The Garden City Utopia: A Critical Biography of Ebenezer Howard* (Macmillan Press, 1988), pp. 86–94, and Patrick Abercrombie, *Greater London Plan* (HMSO, 1944).

14 William Morris, *News from Nowhere and Other Writings*, ed. Clive Wilmer (Penguin Classics, 1993), pp. 61, 77.

15 Ibid., p. 122.

16 I have witnessed this myself, on such projects as Sitopia Farm in Greenwich and Growing Communities in Hackney.

A Radical Shift
Visual Collaboration with Squint Opera

Indy Johar

Alongside the other major cities of the world, London is in a moment of super-large-scale disruptive transformation. This will happen at every level and in many ways simultaneously, although political leaders and citizens are not yet registering its scale. At a fundamental level, the London of today is not suitable for producing the quality of environment that is required for human beings to develop in a positive way throughout the rest of the century, especially in the age of machine learning.

We are still effectively living in the slums we are familiar with from earlier times; it's just that the slums now are different and invisible. Air pollution, light pollution and noise pollution create a constant background that disturbs our health, disconnects us from the world around us, and leads to high cortisol in the body, which induces stress. Food systems take in more energy than they give, while the quality of food – in terms of micronutrients – has long been in decline. Climate change will disrupt global food networks, and there aren't enough materials to retrofit all the buildings we so desperately need to. Almost everything around us will – and must – change.

London has gone through dramatic transformations before, particularly after the Second World War. The problem now is that we've become locked into a theory of incrementalism that ignores the current reality and the structural transition that will happen over the next forty years, as we pass through a period of biomaterial-energy and demographic constraints. London was once a city of many villages that has slowly transformed into a city focused on a central business district, and we might have to reverse that. The city must face up to its challenges, because if it fails to do so, there is a strong possibility that it will diminish in importance. In a way, the brilliance of London lies in its fragility, but unfortunately, it seems that this fragility is increasing and so is its volatility. Thanks to Brexit, the capital is no longer the centrepiece of the European Union or the magnet for human capital that it once was. We've lost a certain ambition. London might build a different story, but this must not happen slowly, and it requires bold leadership.

The scale of what is currently envisaged is just not appropriate for the issues in question. But everything is possible. We must approach the problem at a 'whole London' level, and do it at speed. We must face up to the reality that the city is not liveable for most people, and that there is a systemic problem. Land values make London suitable only as a place for the super-rich to store their wealth, or perhaps for high-value-production economies, but those do not lead to the creation of wealth in other ways. London will have to think long and hard about repositioning itself over a short time.

The energy system will transform massively. Regrettably, enough hydrocarbon energy (from fossil fuels) is not being produced to mine the materials required to retrofit all the city's buildings. Instead, we must start living differently. Now let's imagine that we're in a cold room wearing a T-shirt – but it's got an integrated electric filament heating system. Or perhaps we're in an unheated workspace, but the table itself produces the warmth, like the Japan *kotatsu*. These solutions bring their own problems, such as condensation, but they show how we can reimagine how we live inside spaces in different ways.

The material economy of London will move away from a system based on generating waste. The quantum of materials must be reduced, and at the same time the size of the intangible economy will have to increase. We will need a circular economy based on biomaterials. This will involve reintegrating London into the economies of its surrounding natural landscapes, such as those in Sussex, Essex and Middlesex. This is vital to making the countryside part of a new holistic

Adaptive wearables
Adapting environments to the individual through technologically activated wearables. All images in this essay were produced using the text-to-image AI platform Midjourney.

system of goods and services, rather than simply a convenient place for the rich to live and the poor to visit.

Over the next twenty to thirty years food systems will be revolutionized as a result not only of climate change, but also of us understanding that food is almost like medicine rather than its current incarnation as junk. As weather patterns alter, global food systems will become increasingly volatile and the breadbasket so familiar today will be lost. There will be a move towards large-scale, water-based aquaponic systems, which are created by merging hydroponic and aquaculture farming techniques. Rewilding will allow us to reinvigorate the precious land we have by returning it to its wild state, thus creating good soil producing food that is dense in micronutrients. This is what I mean by thinking of food as a pharmaceutical product. The pharmaceutical industry has become problematic, but at its best it can invent products that have the greatest possible positive impact on human health.

To achieve all of the above will involve a huge and unprecedented investment in human development. Current programmes are still grounded in schools and universities built on fulfilling the requirements of an industrial economy by building a commandable

Biomaterial architecture
As finite resources dwindle, we will cultivate the housing and materials of tomorrow.

Biodiverse food systems
A glade rich in wild herbs and vegetables being studied by a team of permaculture robots.

workforce. How do you create a new economy that will be driven by the need for creativity, complexity and craft intelligence? To do so, new forms of automation will need to be created, alongside greater investment in human development. We must remove the 'bullshit jobs' that nobody wants to do.[1] As well as reducing our material demands in many ways, this will transform the relationship between human and machine in economic terms.

Contemporary London has been driven by the acceleration of consumption – optimized by ever smaller houses and pockets of public realm – and we have to change our priorities. How would our city look as an eight million-person Cambridge or Oxford, a place for deep work and quiet reflection? To create this, how do we start to build a different theory of value, one that isn't about the hustle and bustle of production and consumption? As a society, we must cultivate the patience for complex innovation. Physical spaces become as critical to mental health as our information environment is. People in urban areas are much more likely than rural dwellers to be diagnosed with mental illness, including schizophrenia, so we must desaturate the noise of London.[2] And what will new ways of living look like? There must be a new beauty in them all. People are scared when things are taken away, but we should embrace a new theory of care and an intangible economy.

This future also requires a shift to face-to-face interaction. The combination of the tactile and multichannel digital communication will determine the shape of the physical environment. We have to build with augmented reality in mind, considering how that will marry all the other dimensions. The transition is therefore not about moving entirely to homeworking, because this is often just another tyranny of bad-quality environments, where people work in isolation without the developmental pathways for learning from peers. We should think instead about the intersection of different modes of working as places of productivity. We might work from home but also have pop-up studios or workspaces where we come together at times. These are moments when we will become massively co-involved, proving that face-to-face culture is a critical part of the asset of employees. This change would represent a new possibility for London to be bold and recognize this as a structural transformation of everything around it.

Deep work
Wandering Epping's halls of deep contemplative thought.

Highlighting the metabolic flows of London rather than its boundaries would challenge the existing form of the city's governance. How do you build a governance structure that operates at the scale of twenty or fifty million people, while also considering the needs of smaller communities? This would require new civic town halls at district level, where governance is about citizen participation, coexisting with parametric governance (facilitated by technology) and the more transparent use of automation. Such approaches would allow us to manage smaller elements of local government without resorting to centralized power, and this would be transformational.

A new London for the rest of the twenty-first century will be born as a result of the confluence of change in many things around us: economy, climate and practices of human development. The scientific and technological solutions will not come from one factor but will instead be part of a collaborative action, which requires genuine transformation. This is where city leadership can play a critical role in galvanizing and creating legitimacy for change. But in order to do that, it has to be able to have honest conversations about the risks and

Pop-up studios
Alternative models of labour and work call for flexible, interchangeable workspaces.

Collective governance
The devolution of power from a central government to a hyperlocal community allows local groups to voice and adapt to local demands.

problems, and get citizens involved in the larger discussion. You have to create an informed sense of collective contribution, and a new kind of politics is vital for this transition. The alternative is a slow demise – and that's what is currently happening.

This provocation is not a warning but an invitation for Londoners to participate, because the city won't be transformed by one actor. The democracy of London requires us all to contribute and shift our expectations of how we live, what we consume and how we imagine the city will work on an everyday level. We have to breathe life into a new London through a deep reimagining of it, not just the consumption of it. I think that's the opportunity we have at this moment. Now we must embrace the hope of a radically better tomorrow, as opposed to dealing only with the fears of today.

Notes

1 See David Graeber, *Bullshit Jobs: A Theory* (Penguin, 2018).
2 Lydia Krabbendam and Jim van Os, 'Schizophrenia and Urbanicity: A Major Environmental Influence – Conditional on Genetic Risk', *Schizophrenia Bulletin*, XXXI/4 (October 2005), pp. 795–9.

City of London Futures

Kat Hanna

There sits on Wood Street, next to the office in which I currently work, a church tower, or the substantial remains of one anyway, the origins of which date back to the Middle Ages. Essentially a traffic island overlooking the back entrances of office buildings, the tower of St Alban presents anyone writing about the City of London with all the metaphors they need: the medieval among the modern, the sacred among the profane, heritage among capitalism.

In fact, the reality is that while a church has stood in that location for more than a thousand years, it has been totally demolished and rebuilt on two occasions, and barely survived in its third reincarnation. St Alban is in many respects an ecclesiastical example of Theseus's Paradox, or, to use a more London-centric reference (from the television sitcom *Only Fools and Horses*), Trigger's Broom: is an object that has had all its component parts replaced still the same object? The tower's continued existence should not be taken as an indication of preservationism. The City of London is no stranger to clearing the old to make way for the new. Between 1830 and 1901, twenty-three churches (eighteen of them built by Sir Christopher Wren) were demolished, many to make way for the buildings and institutions that both fuelled and were fuelled by the wealth of empire.[1]

That the City of London is, in built environment terms, full of contrast and idiosyncrasy is not a new observation. By spending any amount of time in the City, it is easy to overlook the remarkable fact that it is built on Roman ruins and encompasses more churches than the Vatican. Familiarity breeds not contempt, but complacency. The narrative of the City that we have shaped is one of its distinctiveness – in its built form, its governance, its history and its habits, as both a basis for and a consequence of its success. The continued presence of such historical oddities as St Alban alongside more recent temples to finance, such as the tower of 22 Bishopsgate, inclines us towards a survivor bias, overlooking instances of limited success or failure.

We tend to skim-read the City's visual history of agglomeration, adaptation and accommodation, and to assume that those forces and behaviours that have driven the City's enduring status will themselves endure, and continue to produce an outcome that looks something like the City as we know it today. This essay, in considering the future of the City of London over the next hundred years, unpacks this area, as it now stands, as having two distinct but overlapping identities: the City as financial services hub and the City as central business district. At the time of writing, we are in a phase when the future of *both* of the City's identities is uncertain. I will focus less on the future of the City of London as an administrative and legislative body, and more on built environment and urbanism. And while it is tempting, when challenged with predicting the future, to retreat into the relative comfort and certainty of the past, this essay will also offer some speculative and not entirely serious scenarios as visions of what may lie ahead.

The City as financial services hub

Its identity as financial services hub is the City that inhabits the imagination of most people – it is both literal and figurative – referring as much to the institutions, their leaders, their decisions and their behaviour as to the physical entity itself. It is this City to which newspaper correspondents refer when discussing economic trends. It is this City, and its institutions regarded as the engines of capitalism, that attracted the opprobrium of assorted groups during the Occupy movement in 2011 around the steps of St Paul's Cathedral: a liminal space in both architectural and cultural terms.

While the City of London's origins are mercantile and religious in equal measure, its identification with financial services is relatively recent. Much has been written of the mutually reinforcing relationship between the City's built environment and its commercial activity. In the words of the historian Michael Hebbert, 'the compactness of a 2,000-year old urban core is fortuitously well suited to the operation of a globalized financial centre.'[2]

Luck, however, is not all there is to it. The City's success as a global financial hub is intrinsically linked to the country's dominance in global trade, in both its origins and its more recent evolution. As the novelist and biographer Peter Ackroyd notes, by 1900 almost half of the world's merchant shipping was controlled, directly or indirectly, by City institutions.[3] The same can be said for the City of London's period of dominance following the 1986 Big Bang (the deregulation of the London stock market), in which a series of policy changes (some UK, some US) saw the United Kingdom establish itself as the world's leading centre for financial services. In both instances, to adopt the description used by the historian Eric Hobsbawm, the City functioned as a 'switchboard' for the world's business transactions.[4]

It is true that the City's compactness played a role in its ability to accommodate a number of financial services institutions and businesses in close proximity to one another. In a textbook example of agglomeration beginning in the mid-nineteenth century, clearing banks sought to be close to the Bank of England as it grew in importance. Ancillary services, such as insurance offices, followed. Few have left since, and many new occupiers have arrived, with the deregulatory period of the late 1980s accelerating the arrival of global capital, businesses and workers. Canary Wharf, developed in the 1990s as a purpose-built rather than 'fortuitous' financial services hub, was briefly considered a competitor to the City as global leader. In reality, despite rhetoric of rivalry, London has to date (before the COVID-19 pandemic, at least) proved itself capable of accommodating more than one financial services hub, particularly in terms of the provision of commercial office space.

The impact of Britain's exit from the European Union, among other macro-economic changes affecting the accumulation and flow of capital, put into question the long-term future of London as *the* global financial centre. This isn't to say that London will simply cease accommodating any financial services activity, but that the status of the City as the pre-eminent

Bloomberg's European headquarters building (2017) in Queen Victoria Street, designed by Foster + Partners.

location could diminish in comparison to that of its heyday, as business, key occupiers and institutions trickle away from the capital. As a result of this process of deagglomeration, it is possible to envisage that the collective hold the City has on our imagination, and not least on its global influence, will gradually weaken and fade. The City may have secured its dominance with the Big Bang, but it's quite possible it will diminish in importance with little more than a whimper.

The City as central business district

Thanks in no small part to its role as financial services hub, the City also represents a major constituent of the capital's central business district (CBD; or, in the parlance of London policymakers and real-estate types, the Central Activity Zone). Not all cities have a 'City', but most have a CBD – that is, a geographical core where certain types of commercial activity, or even a range of them, dominate other uses. To make matters slightly more confusing, although the City may be a CBD, London's CBD is generally considered to extend beyond the City itself to include such surrounding areas as Fitzrovia, the West End and London Bridge, and, as a function of business activity rather than contiguous geography, Canary Wharf.

Definitions and boundaries aside, the notion of the City of London as CBD captures several aspects of its identity. This includes its physical centrality to the capital as a whole, and its concentration of commercial activity, expanding beyond financial services not only into the traditional sectors of insurance, law and property, but also into more recent additions, such as technology and media. There's a smattering of fun too, of course, with the City of London Corporation making a concerted attempt to boost the area's cultural offering through major projects, such as the Museum of London's reopening as The London Museum in Smithfield in 2026, alongside more tactical public-realm interventions, such as the annual Sculpture in the City, a free open-air art exhibition.

The City's identity as CBD also reflects its role as the capital's centre of employment. Of interest here, particularly when thinking about the future of London as a whole, is how the City relates to the rest of the capital, and, indeed, the Southeast. Would we have today's public transport network and suburbs without the City as the centre of gravity? Certainly not the Waterloo and City line, which was opened in 1898 with the primary purpose of speeding the transit of the tens of thousands of commuters who arrived at Waterloo station each day and made their way by horse-drawn bus to the City of London.

Of the challenges to the City's twin identities, this is perhaps the most existential, particularly when it comes to the built form of the area, and its relationship with its surroundings. A City of London that is no longer the leading global financial hub is more conceivable than a City of London that is no longer defined by its predominant activity of 'business', be that even in the broadest sense of the word.

We have plenty of reasons to believe that the City can withstand changes to the type of business activity that it accommodates. To understand its capacity for adaptation, one must look only at the response to the Big Bang and the transition to electronic banking in catalysing the addition of 370,000 square metres (4 million square feet) of office space to the City in the 1980s. Equally, investors and landlords in the City are more than willing to embrace innovation and new technology to better accommodate business. The Lloyd's building was one of the first to adopt internal electric lighting.

But it took a global pandemic and a government-mandated lockdown for us really to question whether the City of London could exist in any relation to its current identity and built form *without* business. It is a question that has been largely disregarded by the City's major stakeholders, be they political, financial or commercial. While the pandemic yielded fanciful and at times fantastical visions of a City abandoned, reclaimed and rendered obsolescent, these were cast aside as the memory of lockdown receded and the Tube carriages filled up once more. Instead, the future of the City of London is one discussed in percentages rather than possibilities: commuter numbers, office occupancies, office vacancies, yields, retail footfall, consumer spend and so on. The debate (if you can call it that) about hybrid working and what it means for the future of the City of London as CBD is really quite homogeneous – and, in its least edifying manifestations, little more than opposing sides of vested interests shouting different numbers at one another. A bit like the trading floor, really.

The focus on considering *where* business activity is carried out as a binary between the City office and the home risks overlooking other, potentially more significant structural changes to the 'business' that currently occupies the City as CBD, particularly if we are to take the hundred-year-long view of this book. It is not feasible here to explore the many ways in which business and work may change over the next twenty years, let alone the next one hundred. How certain can we be either that the City will be able to keep up with the evolution of business and work, or that the concept of work will even be meaningful in the context of our current urban environment?

SCENARIO 1
London as city state

It's 2040. After years of campaigning, London is now an independent city state, having seceded from the United Kingdom after the country's third failed attempt to rejoin the European Union. With the UK Parliament now relocated to Warrington, Cheshire, and the former Houses of Parliament converted into a hotel by an Asian developer, London's Parliament now sits in what was once the Bloomberg Building in the City. No one could ever really get to the Mayor of London's office at Canning Town anyway, and after a period of tense negotiations, a bicameral London Parliament was set up, comprising the mayor and elected London Assembly members in one chamber, and the City of London in a second.

The year 2040 marks the tenth anniversary of London's independence, and five years since the city state rejoined the European Union. Bank Junction, since renamed Independence Circus, plays host to a weekend of anniversary celebrations. This marks a rare appearance for the ceremonial dress of the City of London Chamber members as the parade makes its way from the Bloomberg Building to the Guildhall.

SCENARIO 2
The City as historic quarter

As the saying goes, if it ain't broke, don't fix it. If it is broke, or at least at risk of breaking, don't fix it either; instead, declare it a UNESCO World Heritage Site and preserve it. That was the approach taken by the City of London in 2035, noting the uniqueness of its historic buildings, and its economic and cultural significance in hosting the highest concentration of financial services workspaces and Pret A Manger food outlets in any European city. The City's prominence as a heritage destination began in the late 2020s. As tourists eventually grew tired of the congestion and the American candy stores of Oxford Street, the lure of the City grew stronger, and policymakers, planners and investors decided to double down and make sure that the City's charm remained intact.

The centrepiece of the Underwriting Room of Lloyd's of London (Richard Rogers Partnership, 1986) is the Lutine bell, salvaged from a ship that foundered in 1799 – the disaster that sealed Lloyd's reputation for honouring insurance claims. 'Not a breeze can blow in any latitude,' wrote a journalist in 1859, 'not a storm can burst ... in any part of the world, without recording its history here.'

On the surface, the City of London still looks like a CBD – and it's certainly still central and still a district. But 'business', at least in the sense that we may recognize it today, has long gone: some to the home, some replaced by artificial intelligence, some overseas and the remainder to Canary Wharf. No longer a centre of production, the City has consumption as its main activity, with an international audience in mind. Having a negligible residential and workday population to provide for, the City of London Corporation is now focused on protecting its historic assets to keep its UNESCO World Heritage Site status – an urban environment that has remained untouched since the 2020s, when the Corporation was declared the party responsible for the World Heritage property.

The owners of The Ned hotel and members' club have acquired the Lloyd's of London building, alongside two outposts in Canary Wharf that used to house offices of the banks Barclays and HSBC. The Guildhall removed the last of its governmental functions, and is now a museum, closely trailing the Doge's Palace in Venice as the most visited former administrative building now serving as a tourist destination.

SCENARIO 3
Diversification delivers

Welcome to the City of London, the capital's newest neighbourhood! It's vibrant! It's dynamic! Look closely, and it's maybe even a village! OK, well, it's definitely not a village, but following a strategy for diversifying and intensifying residential use, the City has proved that there *is* life after the CBD.

At a time when CBDs in many cities have struggled to find their feet in a post-'work' world, the City's transition to mixed-use urban neighbourhood continues. More than 10,000 homes have been added to the City's building stock in the past decade, increasing the residential population from 8,000 in 2022 to 20,000 in 2040. Most of these are build-to-rent (BtR) – the result of commercial developers diversifying into residential operations, or, in many instances, partnering with established BtR providers to do so. The City of London is itself developing and managing affordable housing programmes across a range of tenures, funded in part by a decision to devolve a proportion of corporation tax to the Greater London Assembly and the City.

Much of this has been delivered through the conversion of commercial buildings – a process that has cost the City and its investors dearly, both financially and architecturally. Retrofit of commercial buildings, whether retaining their existing use or converting to residential, has resulted in a variety of design outcomes. Walking around the City, it's clear to see which landlords chose to opt out of the City's Retrofit Scheme (CRS) and front the costs themselves; the substantial investment required has now been absorbed by the premium rents paid by occupiers who have embraced the City's diversification away from financial services. Elsewhere, the hallmarks of the CRS are visible in the buildings' façades and materials.

In some instances, CRS-branded hoarding has remained in place for years as the construction sector catches up with retrofit demand. Some people are waiting for the ten-year moratorium on new development to lift in 2045 (with an exemption for social infrastructure, such as schools), following an agreement between the Mayor of London and the City of London Corporation to channel all planning and development resources to retrofit.

Notes

1 Emma Duncan, 'Special Report: On a High', *The Economist*, 28 June 2012, www.economist.com/special-report/2012/06/28/on-a-high.

2 Cited in Peter Ackroyd, *London: The Biography* (Chatto & Windus, 2000), p. 766.

3 Ibid., p. 717.

4 Eric Hobsbawm, *Industry and Empire: From 1750 to the Present Day* [1968] (The New Press, 1999), p. xiii.

Back to the Future
of Architectural Education

Neal Shasore

The founders of The London Society were a motley crew of progressives drawn from the architectural world and wider civil society. Although their political affinities may have varied, they were motivated by shared and broadly liberal ideals. There was therefore a degree of consensus motivating the Society's early supporters who contributed to *London of the Future* in 1921. Their reformist impulses were very much in the spirit of discussion about social, cultural and physical reconstruction in the immediate years following the First World War. These early advocates of The London Society were patricians keen to preserve the role of civil society in urban governance, and were responding in sometimes conflicted ways to the ongoing challenges of industrialization. There was a commitment to strengthening the imperial role of the capital to remake it as a neater, brighter city on a grander scale. And there was a high alertness to the particular challenges of a more widely enfranchised mass democracy in shaping contemporary life, of how to channel competing demands in the design of urban space and to override the hegemony of vested interests (especially those of the railway companies) and the *laissez-faire* attitudes that had underpinned the Victorians' perceived destructive interventions in the city. These anxieties and concerns played out in the early *causes célèbres* of the Society – the campaign to rationalize the arterial roads and surrounding development now encircling the capital, plus the question of the development of the 'Surrey' (south) side of the river and the connected issue of cross-river communication, especially the proposals for new bridges at St Paul's, Waterloo and Charing Cross. What united the disparate politics and visions of the early members of The London Society and contributors to our predecessor volume was a belief in what they conceived as the 'New London' – a capitol fit to serve as the centre of the British Empire and global trade: a sanitized, rationalized, *planned* and *modern* city.

As the historical geographer David Gilbert has argued, The London Society operated as a kind of 'think-tank' provocatively and propositionally engaged in 'futurology'.[1] Indeed, before the First World War, Aston Webb (the Society's first chairman) had prefigured – or more accurately dreamed – his vision of 'London of the Future' in a talk to the Society: bored by the pessimism of a fictional interlocutor, he fell asleep and conjured up more pleasant visions of a cleaner, brighter London, with new axial, arterial routes, an 'Imperial Parliament' and a green girdle around the city.

The conceit of a reverie to paint an optimistic vision of progress was, of course, well established in the nineteenth century. William Morris famously used it for his novella *News from Nowhere*, which was serialized in the Socialist League's publication *Commonweal* in 1890. Morris subverted the emerging genre of science fiction, which fetishized industrial progress and the triumph of the machine (he had critically reviewed Edward Bellamy's utopian novel of 1888, *Looking Backward*, for example), imagining a more pastoral vision of the future of London. *News from Nowhere* was a book that Webb and his architectural contemporaries – many of them Arts and Crafts architects by instinct, but who had 'gone classical' (faintly analogous to when the musician Bob Dylan went electric in 1965) – would have known well.

Morris's short story describes its protagonist – William Guest – returning home from a Socialist League meeting, falling into a deep sleep and waking in the year 2052. The book charts a journey, emotionally and physically, through London and then up the Thames, based on the author's own progress from his town house, Kelmscott House in Hammersmith, to Kelmscott Manor, his Oxfordshire base depicted in the frontispiece of *News from Nowhere* when it was published in full in 1892 by Morris's Kelmscott Press. But Morris's vision of 2052 seemed more to resemble 1552; as Guest traverses central London – in search of an elderly sage,

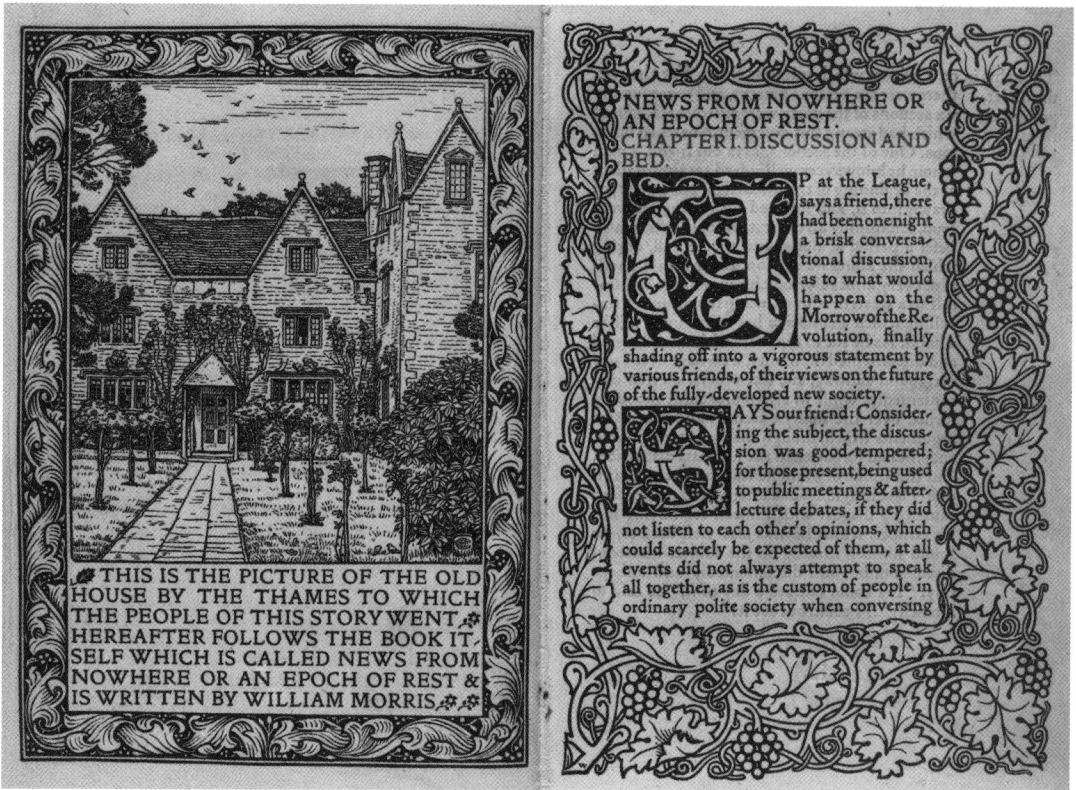

An illustration of a house and garden by Charles March Gere in *News from Nowhere* (1892) by William Morris.

Hammond, to fill in the details of the previous century and a half – he observes a radically decentralized, deindustrialized, deurbanized London – not quite a 'utopia', or a 'non-place', but instead a strangely familiar topography reimagined through Morris's Romantic Socialism. His deeply anti-statist politics is manifest, for example, in the book's dilapidated Palace of Westminster, reduced to a 'Dung Market', a barely metaphorical shit-pile in place of a legislature. Kensington Gardens is the mere tip of a great wood – presumably a reimagining of 'Caen' or 'Ken' Wood – stretching from Paddington eastwards to Primrose Hill, beyond to Stoke Newington and onwards to the Lea Marsh. 'Shopping' – the buying and selling of commodities – is utterly alien to the new society of the twenty-first century, and Piccadilly has been restored to a street of propriety and fine wares. The British Museum, the great monument to modern thinking and rational knowledge, is a ruin – 'the railings were gone, and the whispering boughs of the trees were all about' – retained, despite its ugliness, because 'it is not a bad thing to have some record of what our forefathers thought a handsome building. For there is plenty of labour and material in it.'[2]

News from Nowhere is almost overwhelmingly prescient in its vision of a more ecologically harmonious and equitable society, built on Morris's socialist principles and practical interests. The British Museum, with 'plenty of labour and material in it', could be superficially read as a manifestation of Morris's famous principles of preservation, the 'anti-scrape' philosophy (resisting aggressively 'purist' restoration according to stylistic ideals, in favour of retaining a layered fabric) that informed the foundation of the Society for the Protection of Ancient Buildings in 1877. But that phrase – 'plenty of labour and material in it' – surely resonates with our current and necessary preoccupation with not just *embodied* energy but also the inequity that drives the sometimes desperate labour conditions involved in the production of the built environment. *News from Nowhere* is a parable of degrowth – its published version took the tranquilizing subtitle 'An Epoch of Rest' – and a reaction to the excesses of industrialization and the relentless euphemizing of its cultural and social consequences. Far from soporific, the vision of the world Morris conjures is revitalizing. While at one time this could have been dismissed as 'Arts and Craftsy', idealistic and nostalgic – even, dare I say it, by some of the early members of The London Society – it's a provocative vision with more currency today perhaps than the visions of a more technocratic, hypercharged urban future we are often presented with.

Since I am a historian who runs a resolutely future-facing institution, the London School of Architecture, you might be unsurprised to sense my affinity with Morris. The founding vision of the school contains an aspiration that people live more fulfilled and more sustainable lives in cities. And in the context of climate emergency, of imminent ecological collapse, amid epidemics of enervation and anxiety, of pandemics caused by degraded ecosystems, we need at least to be able to reconceptualize radically how urban life and experience, even in such megacities as London, might look. So what follows is not intended to be Luddite – this is not a manifesto for technophobes – but I want to use this essay as an opportunity to test the possibilities of how a built environment education subtly informed by the traditions of thought that Morris was engaged with might look.

Reading *News from Nowhere* and other of Morris's writings – looking back to look forwards – has its place in current times, in other words.

I invoke Morris to create space for alternative 'future Londons', ones that might not accept the inexorable 'progress' and development of the (post-) industrial city, the bases of which can sometimes feel like an attempt to harness impulses and tendencies to extract, exploit and maximize, rather than engage more fundamentally with the kind of world we might like to live in. And there is perhaps a mild implicit criticism of the patrician liberalism of Aston Webb and many of his contributors, who were born of a particular world view, and the need to introduce a counter-narrative, a voice or a sensibility that is perhaps sceptical of what Webb's vision tacitly endorsed: there are powerful synergies between the contradictions of the new liberal vision of the city that The London Society espoused and the neoliberal mainstream forces of development today. Writing about a vision of education places you perhaps at one remove from the actual remaking of the city. But creating an educational framework and a pedagogy that can challenge the minds of those we are teaching to effect the change London will need – whether it likes it or not – is significant.

I propose an educational framework supported by three strong pillars:

1   To decolonize, decarbonize and destandardize design – to take these imperatives as provocations rather than projects, and to understand the basic epistemic questions they pose for educating those involved in the production of the built environment.
2   To embed a 'meaningful municipalism' in our practices – to connect design with new and resurgent forms of political action and intervention, and to build on educational models that are rooted in civic agency and civil society.
3   To build these ideals into a 'built environment fellowship' – to foster a common educational framework across design, development and construction focusing on collaboration, mutual respect, and inter- and multidisciplinary knowledge to create a safe, sustainable and socially inclusive built environment.

Decolonize, decarbonize and destandardize

London of the Future in 1921 was conceived as a modernized, imperial metropolis: the seat of an imperial legislature, and a city to rival Continental capitals and the grandest exemplars of the American 'City Beautiful' movement in urban planning. Empire was inscribed into the existing London through axial routes, street names, statues and street furniture.

These comprised the spatial tools and visual codes of coloniality: Regent Street, rebuilt on Crown land in the first quarter of the twentieth century, was considered an imperial thoroughfare exemplifying the commercial hub of consumerism. The artist Stephen Bone's mural at Piccadilly Circus Underground station showed it as a 'Hub of Empire'. The Strand–Aldwych development incorporated new High Commissions for Australia and India. At Wembley the British Empire Exhibition of 1924 brought concrete monumentality to the suburban domesticity of 'metroland' in the name of promoting trade within the British Empire. As the engineer John Rennie's old Waterloo Bridge was demolished, 'relics' of the old fabric – stone blocks, balustrades, timber piling – were distributed to the far-flung corners of the empire as mementos (or architectural *memento mori*), tangible links to the heart of the British imperium.

There were, in other words, complex ways in which coloniality was written into London's present and future in the early twentieth century. Why, then, is it so difficult to conceive of *decolonizing* London in the future now? Or rather, how might decolonial thinking open up new possibilities for spatial production and spatial justice in the city?

In sum, decoloniality seeks to dismantle Eurocentrism – to bring again into existence ideas about living and being in the world that were lost through colonial violence. Although it has been framed as *destructive* in public discourse, it is in fact fundamentally *constructive*, or reconstructive: seeking to re-energize, rebuild, re-engage human life in closer harmony with nature (in fact to collapse the artificial construct of 'nature' versus 'culture'), to unpick patriarchal and racist structures, to promote plurality of thought, and to embrace diverse ways of thinking, knowing, living, being and feeling. Far from fetishizing or primitivizing the precolonial, it encourages reconnection to and celebration of productive and regenerative ideas in our many heritages and histories, and in the Indigenous world views that were suppressed through colonial expansion. In a city where, in 2023, 42 per cent of the population are of Asian, Black, mixed or other ethnic origin – many of whom have links only one or two generations back to actual or former colonies of the British or other empires – such an approach could be transformative not just in built environment education but also in learning and pedagogy broadly. In the case of what we call architectural education – a Eurocentric construct of professional practice – this does not mean simply 'translating' ideas from other places and times into the contemporary conventions of design, but understanding different ways

William Richard Lethaby's unexecuted scheme for Kingsway, *c.* 1900.

of holding and developing land, of surveying it, of building on it, of living and being in space, on their own terms.

Decolonial thought has real currency for the climate emergency, which is as much a psychological, even ontological, crisis, as a technical problem to solve. Nevertheless, as Architects Climate Action Network (ACAN) has argued, decarbonizing construction, first through regulating embodied carbon as well as operational carbon, is an urgent imperative.[3] We need to develop new forms of teaching that embrace these new realities – that use drawing and making to make energy's immanence more immediately visible and legible. We must be bolder in reforming some of the basic assumptions underwriting our curricula.

Again, we can look backwards to look forwards: these were precisely the arguments that the architect, reformer and educationalist William Richard Lethaby was mobilizing even in the 1890s, writing that:

> The art of architecture is ... the co-ordination of the several crafts in the achievement of right or beautiful building; and this not only in the outer form and adornment, but in the very structure and anatomy. Architecture is the easy and expressive handling of materials in masterly experimental building – it is the craftsmen's Drama.

He went on, quoting Morris:

> Too often what the modern practitioner has produced 'is not a building which really forms part of the living shell and skin of the earth on which we live, but is a mere excrescence upon it, a toy which might almost as well, except for the absolute necessities of the people having a roof to cover them, have remained simply a nicely executed drawing in the architect's office.'[4]

Morris wrote lyrically in *News from Nowhere* of the 'spirit of the new days, of our days' as 'delight in the life of the world; intense and overweening love of the very skin and surface of the earth on which man dwells'.[5] This underpins an aspiration for sustainable and regenerative building practice.

And finally we must find new ways of teaching that acknowledge the need for, and enable, a built environment for all, especially in relation to physical disability and neurodiversity. Teaching should challenge the constructed norms of bodily experience, and should question the basic premises of standards and standardization often born of a belief in the 'universal' and singular.

Meaningful municipalism

The vision of *London of the Future* in 1921 was of a modern megacity – replanned and reordered. That seam of thinking later manifested in, for example, the Royal Academy Planning Committee's vision of London's reconstruction during and after the Second World War. The architect and urban planner Lionel Brett derided it as 'the New Haussmann', mocking its affinities to the reconstruction of Paris under Emperor Napoleon III in the second half of the nineteenth century.[6] There were other visions of the city, which have had an enduring imaginative hold – the Danish architect

Steen Eiler Rasmussen's *London: The Unique City* (1934) talks of many little Londons, of interconnected villages with distinct histories and characters.

But at a more profound level there has been a translocal revival of more radical municipalist politics with attendant economic theory and socio-cultural formations. For Generation Z, let down as it has been by the political machinations of the nation-state, to think of politics primarily at a more local or civic scale has its attractions. The Fearless Cities movement, inspired by the libertarian socialist and environmentalist Murray Bookchin, gives examples of engaged and distributive participatory politics, popular assemblies and more equitable visions of urban life. As they put it, their mission is 'to radicalize democracy, feminize politics and drive the transition to an economy that cares for people and our environment.'[7] There is no singular definition of municipalism and how it might work, but nor has there been a significant exploration of how it might shift the morphology of our cities. There are, however, initiatives that are beginning to show the way: the Southwark Land Commission launched in early 2023 explores the radical devolution of power to communities to shape their corner of the city for the public good, building on the work of community land trusts (non-profit organizations that own, manage and develop land for the benefit of the community).

Multilateral action is absolutely needed in the face of climate emergency, but if extractivism was a tactic of the (imperial) nation-state, it is at least questionable that the nation-state will be able to get us out of the very messes that it first made. Civil society empowered by volunteerism and associational culture always runs the risk of lapsing into the kind of patrician philanthropy and do-gooding that motivated the first members of The London Society in the early twentieth century – advocating for a more meaningful and radical municipalism in the early twenty-first may restore some faith in political agency. It would not only allow us to question how land and development could be put better into service of environmental and social justice, but also provide a new frame for how we conceive of the structure of our industry and industrial relations in shaping the production of the built environment.

Built environment fellowship

The Grenfell Tower Inquiry (examining the circumstances leading up to and surrounding the devastating fire at Grenfell Tower on 14 June 2017) identified a 'web of blame'. This weaves together incompetence across the span of construction and development, up and down the nooks and crannies of the supply chain, from architects to engineers, governmental bodies, product manufacturers and specialist subconsultants. The engineer Dame Judith Hackitt's independent review of building regulations and fire safety in 2018 called for a fundamental rethink of the system and how it works, echoing similar calls for reform of the often irrational and internecine construction industry going back nearly a century. Demands for educational reform tend, however, to be siloed or even born of professional self-interest. Bold thinking about a common educational framework across the building industry and wider built environment sector has been lacking. This could be generated by a conception of a 'built environment fellowship', as others (such as the Edge Commission) have coined it – an ideal of mutual respect, common language and shared learning. 'Fellowship' is fundamental, not just incidental to this: 'Fellowship is life, and lack of fellowship is death,' as Morris put it, after all.[8]

A renewed ideal of 'built environment fellowship' could catalyse three elements in the regeneration of London and the reorganization of education across development and construction. First, it could drive a common foundational educational framework across the construction industry, one unshackled from the outdated professional manacles it was forced into in the nineteenth century, and one that connects to wider shifts in technical education. Tinkering with existing structures will have limited impact unless we think across disciplines. As we move towards lifelong learning, we could then define multiple, accessible and affordable educational routes across the span of a career, responding to industrial and economic need as people train, retrain and specialize with greater ease. A common, foundational educational framework could foster mutual understanding and respect, and re-establish not so much the basic standards of development, but a basis for the flourishing of life of all kinds on the planet.

In order to implement this, we need to understand the desirable career and learning pathways for the underserved and underrepresented communities in the wider sector, as well as for those already participating in built environment educational programmes. We also need to develop the means of assessing sector skills shortages – the immediate needs, as well as green skills and climate literacy – at a local level, while developing a clearer vision of the economic need of industry and the distribution of construction in the wider region. We should be leveraging social value and other contributions to development to provide a financial underpinning for the resulting programmes we design at this foundational level in technical education. This will strengthen, and perhaps make more legible, what we already have: an increasingly diverse set of learning opportunities in design and construction (T-levels, Higher Technical Qualifications, Foundations, Higher and Degree Apprenticeships, and so on). Our industrial partners and representatives should come together to review apprenticeship standards and other qualifications and routes to entry.

Second, a conception of built environment fellowship could underpin the reorganization of the construction industry and wider built environment sector in the service of the public good. We will be able to identify and enrich roles and responsibilities that are responsive to new technology, methods and regulatory frameworks, that are highly competent, and that think more holistically of the city, its systems and flows. A more united and better-integrated built environment sector will be able to advocate more effectively for better spaces and places in the city.

Third, as a corollary, the argument for a just transition to a green economy would be stronger: there would be a basis for improving labour conditions across the construction industry, recognizing and remunerating all forms of work involved in the production of the built environment. Some in the professions may balk at the idea of a built environment fellowship – may, indeed, fear a 'watering down' or 'dumbing down' as an unintended consequence – but with more joined-up thinking and higher standards globally, the quality of education could improve dramatically.

These 'visions' – visions like Morris's – might seem naively idealistic, divorced from reality. And they require more pragmatic minds to work out the detail. Morris certainly had his: W.R. Lethaby was an affirmed disciple of Morris's writings and ideals. He sought to put into practice – and into pedagogy – what have become the clichés of the philosophy of Morris and the writer John Ruskin: of joy in labour, of craft and making as fundamental to architecture, of the re-enchantment, even resacralization of life in tune with the cosmos and with nature, and of what we now call resilience and endurance in design, and so on. But Lethaby was deeply practical too, serving as the art inspector to the Board of Technical Education instigated by the London County Council (the predecessor to our Greater London Authority). He built up the Central School of Arts and Crafts (now part of Central Saint Martins) and promoted the new Brixton School of Building intended to integrate architecture with the building trades. Lethaby, via Morris, presents a still more radical alternative vision of the future than

Webb and his contemporaries perhaps envisioned. Lethaby, like Morris, was a prophet – or, perhaps more prosaically, he saw what futures conventional wisdom would inevitably chart. This is Lethaby on the dangers of what he called the 'paper-architect':

> It is the very mission of such an architect to teach the builder and workman his proper place and due ignorance ... If you want to learn architecture, you must study architecture – that is, architectural construction, not the gymnastics which will overlap the building act. You must pry into material. You must learn the actual 'I know' of the workman. Work manually at a craft – if you begin with one you will end with many – not with a view of gaining what is called 'practical experience', but to gain the power of real artistic expression in material.[9]

This feels like a particularly valuable insight for a post-Grenfell construction industry, far from the hedonistic fetish of a cladding system conceived at such remove from making, calling fundamentally for an architecture rooted in knowledge of materials.

In our response to the twin crises of climate change and inequity we need a renewal of our educational models across the built environment. To think within largely nineteenth-century professional parameters would be misguided and a wasted opportunity; we need a more ambitious conception of how our environments are made and sustained, of the imbrication of built and natural environments.

Notes

1 David Gilbert, 'London of the Future: The Metropolis Reimagined after the Great War', Journal of British Studies, XLIII/1 (January 2004), pp. 91–119.

2 William Morris, News from Nowhere, ed. Krishan Kumar (Cambridge University Press, 1995, repr. 2002), pp. 53–4.

3 See www.architectscan.org/action.

4 W.R. Lethaby, 'The Builder's Art and the Craftsman', in Architecture: A Profession or an Art?, ed. R.N. Shaw and T.G.

Jackson (John Murray, 1892), pp. 151, 156.

5 Morris, News from Nowhere, p. 135.

6 Lionel Brett, 'The New Haussmann: Royal Academy Planning Committee's Plans for London', Architectural Review, XCIII (January 1943), pp. 23–5.

7 See www.fearlesscities.com/about.

8 William Morris, A Dream of John Ball (Delphi Classics, 2015), n.p.

9 Lethaby, 'The Builder's Art', pp. 154, 164–5.

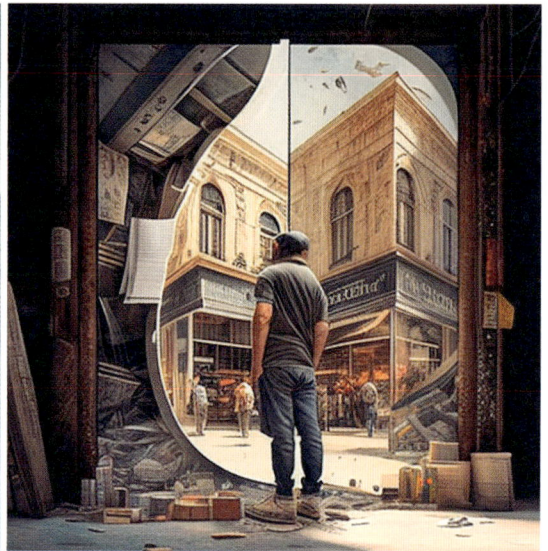

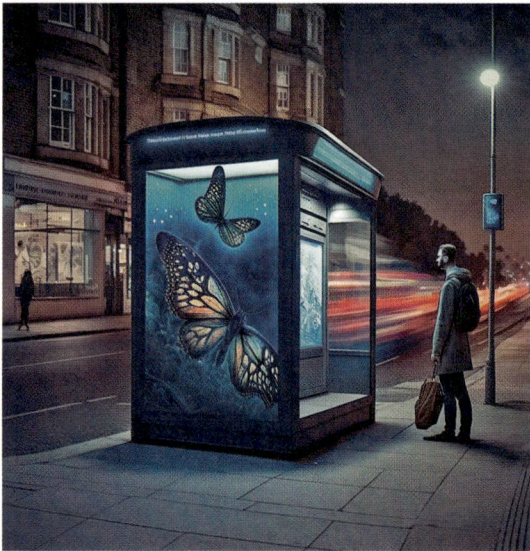

Visions for AI-led culture generated using Midjourney in March 2023.

A Leap of Imagination

Jude Kelly

What will London's culture look like in one hundred years' time? Will we still be a global capital of creativity or will the climate crisis have fundamentally reconfigured the city's ways of operating? Predictions are the business of fortune-tellers, political pundits and financial markets (and we all know how reliable they are). Despite this, conjuring up ideas, dreaming and breaking the mould are what the arts do best, so I write this in the knowledge that sometimes you just have to will things into being through fervour and faith.

I hope that London will be a place that delivers a creative life for all its citizens. I hope it strives to expand the imagination of society in a powerful and positive way. I hope it commits to inducing deeper empathy and a conscious desire to realize every person's potential. I hope it adds the arts to the list of things communities can always expect to have in their midst.

This book is inspired by its predecessor from 1921. So let us start our journey into the future by looking back a hundred years to conversations that caught fire then. One day in 1920 the young Czech writer Karel Čapek sought the advice of his older brother Josef, a painter. Karel was writing a play about non-human workers but was struggling for a name for them. 'I'd call them *labori*, after the Latin root *labor*, but that seems too bookish,' he told Josef, who was hard at work on a canvas. 'Call them *roboti*, then,' replied his brother, drawing on the Old Church Slavonic word *robota*, meaning 'servitude', 'forced labour' or 'drudgery'. Thus was the word 'robot' introduced into language. The Slavonic word, also common in German, Russian and Polish, was a product of the central European system of serfdom by which a tenant's rent was paid for in forced labour or service. Čapek's play, *R.U.R.* (or *Rossum's Universal Robots*), is set in the year 2000 and prophetically imagines how technological progress will come to dominate the world. Robots are cheap, easily available and able to produce goods at a fifth of the cost of human production. The pressure is for ever greater productivity and higher dividends to investors. However, the League of Humanity pleads the robots' case, saying that they should be paid for their work and be given a 'soul', or they are effectively enslaved. Unfortunately, it doesn't end well for humans. Čapek is positing the question of whether nature, thought, initiative, imagination and soul are being substituted for profitability.

R.U.R. was an instant success. By 1923 it had been translated into thirty languages, and by 1927 it was so popular that the BBC aired it as one of its first radio dramas. At the same moment that *R.U.R.* was being written, a Russian writer named Yevgeny Zamyatin was writing *We*, a novel about a high-tech future dictatorship. *We* is set in One State, an urban nation constructed almost entirely of glass, which assists in mass surveillance. There is no way of referring to people except by their given numbers, and the society is run strictly by logic or reason as the primary justification for its laws and customs. Dreams are thought to be a symptom of mental illness. Like *R.U.R.*, *We* was celebrated, and after reading it, George Orwell began his novel *Nineteen Eighty-four*, acknowledging *We* as a model.[1]

A century ago these writers gave us robots and the mechanized dystopia, the concept of which, it seems, will never die. A hundred years on and many cutting-edge creative conversations are still about the mystery and fears surrounding robots' capabilities. London is now considered by the majority of the arts and tech community to be the European epicentre for talent in artificial intelligence (AI). In 2022 I gave a speech as part of CogX in London's King's Cross, a conference described as 'the largest gathering of creative minds looking at challenges and tech-based solutions'.[2] Thousands of people gathered to explore the next threshold of potential for Web3 (a decentralized version of the World Wide Web), the metaverse, NFTs (non-fungible tokens, or unique digital identifiers), and the advancement of robotics and AI.

People who queried some of the discussions or tried to raise the alarm about this fascination with robotics were viewed by many as Luddites, rather like those who thought the internet was never going to amount to much. The focus on the sunny uplands was the overall philosophical position of this young urban audience, and there's no reason to scorn that. After all, each generation takes pride in its role in adopting change and normalizing the new. However, artists' warnings concerning our love of AI are not intended to stop technological advancement in its tracks, but to remind us that progress in the capital should be focused on people and community rather than machines, avatars and algorithms. This sense of justice, compassion and equality – plus a shared sense of joy and community aspiration – releases energy and ambition that are visceral, dynamic and the true stuff of human progress. But they are far harder to achieve and require a constant act of faith. As one of Čapek's characters says in his novel *The Absolute at Large* (1922), 'the greater the things are in which a man believes, the more fiercely he despises those who don't believe in them. And yet the greatest of all beliefs would be belief in one's fellow-men.'[3] In the end, I think it is always people and not technology that shape a great capital city.

This is why I draw attention to other conversations that were taking place a hundred years ago in London about the role face-to-face art and culture could play in this act of human advancement. In the 1920s the legendary theatrical producer Lilian Baylis had transformed the Old Vic theatre and was embarking on acquiring the derelict Sadler's Wells for the nation, fuelled by her belief in achieving social progress through the arts. Her commitment to access to culture had a marked impact on the working-class areas her theatres served. One commentator wrote: 'In every direction there is a longing to rise out of all that is low and sordid and ugly. Who can tell what it may foreshadow in the future to put the best form of entertainment within reach of those who are already seeking higher things?'[4]

At Baylis's behest the former Ballets Russes dancer Ninette de Valois was leading a new dance company that eventually relocated to Covent Garden and became the Royal Ballet. Baylis's Sadler's Wells opera performances in English became the English National Opera at the Coliseum. Her company of actors at the Old Vic – including Laurence Olivier, Peggy Ashcroft, John Gielgud, Edith Evans and Ralph Richardson – later formed the National Theatre. And in creating three of the great London cultural institutions, she also laid down a gauntlet for the future. She gave away free tickets to local families, she ran play days for young people, and she lobbied for the education system to recognize the right of children to have the arts in their lives from an early age. Only a few hundred years before, it was still assumed that few people could or should read and write. It was also believed that artistic activity and enjoyment were the province of the élite members of society. Gradually the needs of the workplace combined with demands for universal education, forcing literacy to become the norm, not the exception. But art and culture remained stubbornly set apart from most people's common experience. Phrases such as 'not for me' and 'not for them' summed up the attitudes that policed access to much of what art had to offer, and reinforced ideas of the specialness or superiority of those who indulged.

Baylis was scornful of that snobbery and of the exclusion of the general population that was desired by many of the artistic élite. She died in 1937, a powerful but still unorthodox voice. Her baton was passed, however unceremoniously, to a London blitzed and near-broken after the Second World War, but that was presented with the astonishing determination of the Festival of Britain in 1951. With a stated aim to provide a tonic for the nation, it flaunted excellence and egalitarianism side by side. The capital's government, the Greater London Council, encouraged the politician and leader of the festival, Herbert Morrison, to dream and then execute a vision for the south bank of the Thames. In place of grimness and squalor a new landscape was constructed.

Morrison had the courage to insist that the south side of the river, 'the poor side', the unglamorous side, with the prison, the asylum and the bad transport, warranted belief and transformation. The new Royal Festival Hall, with its rooftop restaurant, the People's Palace, welcomed crowds from everywhere to wander into its huge foyers and back out to the fountains, gardens and pop-up cafés. For only a few months, this festival vista modelled a celebration of peace and inclusion that underlined the reasons for fighting a war. It used art and culture to speak about a world in which joy, curiosity and human talent trumped brute power and superiority.

Some of the artists who worked on this vision were refugees, many of whom were escaping the Holocaust. They knew that the freedom to express and see themselves and their stories represented gives a person true dignity and equality. Many of those refugees went into broadcasting, publishing, concert promotion and film. They helped to shape the greatness of London as a creative powerhouse. They helped to mould both the highbrow and the middlebrow. They wanted to contribute greatly to the society that had opened its arms to them. Many wanted to extend that sense of inclusion to others.

This was the period when evangelist types fought to widen access in every way possible: establishing concert halls, museums, galleries, theatres, art schools, and dance and drama colleges; teaching the arts in primary and secondary education; founding the Arts Council to widen distribution and participation; and constantly challenging the tiresome trope that wider access equals dumbing down. Another great figure appeared on the London scene to further disturb the complacency the arts still displayed, to challenge the idea that the arts are a luxury belonging to the educated and the Establishment. This was the theatre director Joan Littlewood. Often described as the 'mother of modern theatre', she believed that the arts should 'reflect the dreams and struggles of the people', and wanted above all to tell the unheard stories of the forgotten working class.[5]

Littlewood's theatre at Stratford, a tough part of a then undeveloped East End, was a huge contrast to the theatreland of the West End. Its philosophy of inclusion kept the pressure on by trying to persuade the sceptics and the puritanical aesthetes that a vigorous creative life must permeate all communities and that the capital city must be boldly idealistic on behalf of the country. Her biggest dream with the architect Cedric Price was to build a Fun Palace on the side of the River Lee that would combine art, technology, education and community, and that was welcoming to everyone. It was never realized, but the vision influenced thousands of outsiders and mavericks of all kinds to insist that their voices should count and, indeed, that their voices might lead.

Jenny Lee, as minister for the arts from 1967 to 1970, took arts access into the political heart of government for the first time. She proselytized the widest possible engagement for the greatest number of people, and pressed for arts funding to reflect this aim. Community arts initiatives of all kinds sprang up and struggled for artistic legitimacy alongside the 'proper arts' that emerged from more classical origins. But the movement to democratize creative expression marched on, pioneered by passionate people who believed in the potential of humans rather than the love of technology. Feminism gave confidence to the insistence on a seat at the creative table for women, and a long-overdue look back at history to acknowledge the forgotten, marginalized or invisible contributions by women.

Clean Break, a theatre company founded by Jacqui Holborough and Jenny Hicks in 1979, and the art therapist Joyce Laing forged new programmes for prisoners seeking rehabilitation. Throughout the 1980s and 1990s pub theatres, spoken word cafés, music venues, film collectives, dance projects and local arts centres provided homes for a plethora of powerful arts and cultural initiatives that reflected the stories and experiences of Black and ethnic minority communities, homeless people, LGBT people, people with disabilities and the ever-changing refugee population – ensuring they were given a platform in real time.

At the turn of the century Chris Smith, a Member of Parliament who was Lee's natural inheritor, used his power as a new cabinet minister with a new government department, the Department for Culture, Media and Sport, to make all state art galleries and museums free of charge. He also compelled the Treasury to acknowledge the scale of financial contribution that the creative industries provide to London in particular.

When London competed to host the 2012 Olympic and Paralympic Games, a major part of our bid revolved around the power of culture to serve as a catalyst for change. As the person leading that part of the bid, I initially found the age-old resistance to focusing on inclusion rather than proven artistic excellence. However, we prevailed with our argument that future London talent would be found in the young, ethnically diverse population of the six Olympic host boroughs, which should become the catalyst for a nationwide intense programme of filmmaking, dance and music production, with training in every aspect of the creative industries. It gave thousands of young Londoners a chance to describe their experiences and shape the future narrative of the city.

I'm constantly excited by human progress, and although I'm aware that improvement isn't linear, it still seems to aim, however waywardly, towards a more equal and respectful society. But understanding the role the arts can play as part of that vision requires us to shift our perspective from seeing them as a luxury to believing them to be fundamental to everyone's everyday life. It also needs a leap of faith and dogged commitment to values that aren't fashionable or newsworthy, but are essential.

What might the cultural life in London 2123 be like, then? I would like to envisage a future inspired by the hyperlocal approach of the twentieth century. We will see the arts as a part of the everyday, within corner shops and bus stops. All schools will contain music and film studios, drama and dance workshops, art and design rooms, and theatre/concert halls. These facilities will be made available for use by the surrounding communities, who will be part of choirs, drama groups, book clubs, film societies and more.

The pub theatre, the arts centre, the library, and the community square for outdoor cinema and entertainment will be a feature of all neighbourhoods. Childcare will be free and all children under the age of five will be able to take part in programmes that ensure music, story-making and art-making happen alongside emotional learning. All people aged under twenty-one and over fifty-five will receive 'London Creative Cards' that give them free travel and tickets for a wide range of shows, projects and classes. The planning laws that call for further public good when redeveloping have resulted in brilliant hybrid arts complexes, where mental and physical health specialists, child development workers, rehab and addiction assistance, dentists, and Citizens Advice (an independent organization providing free, independent and confidential advice) are all housed alongside arts amenities of many different types.

AI *will* be a major provider of cultural consumption in the future, but it will support individual social reformers, insisting that the human side, which will redescribe London in ways that truly transform, prospers. This prediction does remind us, though, that less than 14 per cent of current researchers into AI are women and that this number is decreasing, which is an interesting parallel with the fact that a hundred years ago women still didn't all qualify to vote. We must ensure that there is equity among those responsible for harnessing the arts if we want the bright future we hope for.

Despite the fact that artists and writers have often predicted a dystopian world of dangerous robots, dark satanic mills and mass surveillance, warning of serfdom in both human and mechanical form, there was also created a different and powerful vision of the possibilities of perfection. Thomas More, living in London in the sixteenth century, coined the word 'utopia' from the Greek *ou-topos* (no place) and thus challenged us to consider the harder route of dignity, pluralism, sharing of resources and compassion. Perhaps we can take inspiration from a figure of 500 years ago to plan out a London in the coming century that embraces the talent that exists on every street corner and celebrates it for the generations to come. Maybe we just need a leap of imagination.

Notes

1 See Gordon Bowker, *Inside George Orwell: A Biography* (Palgrave Macmillan, 2003), p. 340; Isaac Deutscher, '1984: The Mysticism of Cruelty', in *George Orwell*, ed. Raymond Williams (Viking Press, 1971), pp. 120–6.

2 See www.cogxfestival.com.

3 Karel Čapek, *The Absolute at Large* (Wildside Press, 2023), p. 171.

4 Quoted in Susie Gilbert, *Opera for Everybody: The Story of English National Opera* (Faber & Faber, 2009), p. 22.

5 'Theatre Workshop', in *The Continuum Companion to Twentieth Century Theatre*, ed. Colin Chambers (Continuum, 2002), p. 773.

Black Lives Matter protest march from Vauxhall to Westminster, June 2020.

Daring to Dream

Baroness Lawrence of Clarendon

We must dare to dream. Not everything I'd like for London can be achieved in the short term. But that's no reason not to hope for it, to do all that we can – no matter how little – to move things in the desired direction, towards a more equitable capital city. The areas in which I would most like to see improvements are housing, education, policing and racial equality.

One of London's main problems is that growing numbers of young people can't afford to live in it. Sometimes they simply don't earn enough, but often, even though they have well-paid jobs, they can't raise the requisite deposit for a house or flat purchase because they pay so much in rent. According to a report in 2019 by the housing charity Shelter, private renters on low incomes spend an average of 67 per cent of their earnings on rent.[1] Not up to 67 per cent: 67 per cent on average. Increasingly, people have no option but to live with their parents into their thirties, sometimes even longer; many of them can't hope to get on to the property ladder unless or until they inherit. Alternatively, even though they work in London, they have to live outside it. They spend so much of their money on transport to and from home that saving becomes hard or even impossible. It was not always this way. How can it be changed?

As with every major difficulty, there's no simple solution; if there were, someone would already have thought of it. 'Affordable housing' is a term that gets bandied about, but it can mean pretty much whatever you want it to mean: affordable by whom? What I'd like to see is more social housing – homes let to tenants at reasonable rents. There's nothing wrong in principle with 'right to buy'; the problem with it, as it was enshrined in the Housing Act (1980), was that no new homes were built to replenish the social housing stock that was sold off into private ownership. Indeed, at that time local councils were actively prevented from building new domestic accommodation, which makes it bitterly ironic that today they get blamed for the lack of such places to live in. I never understood why the government (1979–90) of Conservative prime minister Margaret Thatcher, having enriched one group of people, didn't create opportunities for others to follow them along the road to prosperity. The great council house sell-off coincided with a recession in the building trade: that has always struck me as needless, wrong and shameful.

If we build more new homes, we will stimulate a range of industries. That seems almost too obvious to need saying, but one of the objections to it you hear is that there's no room in London. Certainly the cost of what little land that is available is very high, but an attractive possible solution is upward extensions to existing buildings. That's the mission of Skyroom, an urban development company that installs new homes, prefabricated offsite, on top of houses and offices within easy reach of hospitals, schools and other places where keyworkers do their jobs. In a perfect world London would be a '15-minute city', in which every resident could make the journey between home and work in no longer than that time, but the people at Skyroom know that that goal is unachievable practically. Nonetheless, they aim to have built 10,000 homes of this type by 2030: it's not a magic bullet, but it's a shot on target.

And it's not enough simply to build more homes: we need to monitor much more closely than of late the methods and materials used in their construction. Otherwise we'll get more disasters such as the 2017 one at Grenfell Tower, the twenty-four-storey high-rise building in North Kensington that caught fire, killing seventy-two people. The blaze was started by an electrical fault in a fourth-floor refrigerator; it spread so quickly and lethally because cladding on the building that should have been flame-resistant was combustible.

A silent march for the victims of the Grenfell Tower fire, held on 14 June 2018, one year after the inferno.

In the aftermath of this tragedy it emerged that cladding of the same type was in place in other high-rise buildings all over the country. It should have been a national priority to replace this material pre-emptively as soon as was humanly possible. However, shortly after the second anniversary of the fire, the Conservative prime minister Theresa May was asked by the Labour Party leader Jeremy Corbyn why there were still 328 high-rise buildings with Grenfell-style cladding. Her reply was as revealing as it was shocking. She said: 'We asked building owners in the private sector to take the action that we believed necessary, but they have not been acting quickly enough. That is why we will fully fund the replacement of cladding on high-rise residential buildings, and interim measures are in place where necessary.'[2]

In such circumstances the government should not be asking for action: it should be commanding it or taking it itself. 'We will fully fund' does not represent leadership; it's prevarication. So too is 'where necessary'. As I write this, more than five years after the Grenfell fire, about 60,000 people are still living in those 328 blocks. Those who own such blighted accommodation can't sell it because no one wants to live in a tinderbox (and even if they did, no one would lend them the money for the mortgage); they cannot afford to undertake the necessary remedial work themselves; they live in constant fear.

Another change I'd dearly like to see is in education: I want to decolonize it. When I was growing up, what I was taught in school did not reflect anything that I or people like me could relate to. That was especially true in history lessons, where we heard plenty about the kings and queens of England and bits about some of the kings of France, but not a word about the Windrush generation or, indeed, the Afro-Caribbean people who lived in Britain hundreds of years before that post-war wave of immigration. And since the schools never taught any of that, it's unsurprising that they also made no mention of the fact that the West Indians who came to the United Kingdom from 1948 onwards (the first of them on the ship *Empire Windrush*) didn't just turn up on a whim; they were sought out and encouraged to come by a British government that was anxious to rebuild after the destruction caused by the Second World War but lacked the people to do the work.

I would like to see schools encourage every pupil to find out and learn about where his or her forebears came from so that, to put it in its plainest terms, if and when people tell you to go back to your own country – even if that's neither desirable nor possible, and even though you quite reasonably resent being insulted like that, not least because you were born here and have always lived here – you need to know where that was. The basis of racism is ignorance, and I believe that the sooner we realize that everyone comes from somewhere else – that we're all immigrants; that the British Isles were once uninhabitable thousands of years ago because they were covered with an ice sheet – the sooner racism will be minimized, perhaps even eradicated.

Altering the syllabus to take account of Britain's effect on other parts of the world would be good for students countrywide, but I think it would be of particular benefit to London because it would help to address one of the city's biggest challenges: the urgent need to strengthen the relationship between its people and its police. Although there are plenty of good, honest officers in the Metropolitan Police, the reputation of the Met as a whole has long been tarnished by high-profile cases of corruption and racism. The names of Sarah Everard (unlawfully arrested, kidnapped, raped and murdered by a serving officer in March 2021) and Nicole Smallman and Bibaa Henry (who were stabbed to death in a London park in June 2020 and then had their bodies photographed by two constables in selfies shared on WhatsApp) will not easily be dislodged from the communal memory. There have been many other scandalous cases. Public trust in the Met has diminished, particularly in Black and ethnic minority communities, but also more widely: today fewer Londoners than ever before take it for granted that the police are reliable agents of fairness.

Once trust goes, consent isn't far behind, and non-consensual policing threatens the very foundations of a free society. I'm not convinced that the Met as currently constituted understand that. I think the force feels embattled – that it's them against us, the people. Such a hostile view of the world can be self-perpetuating: it may be inculcated into new recruits – young men and women who have neither the formal education nor the life experience to realize that a warrant card does not bestow limitless power on the holder. The Met today are like an open sore that can't be healed because they make no attempt

New Scotland Yard on Victoria Embankment, the headquarters of the Metropolitan Police.

really to heal it. A lot of learning needs to be undertaken if they don't want to still be seen as a corrupt and racist organization in a hundred years' time.

While recognizing that there are no easy fixes to complex difficulties, I am concerned that as a society we are increasingly making grand statements of intent and then doing little or nothing to action them. The response to Grenfell is one example; another is our approach to race relations. Published in 1999, the Macpherson Report on the handling of the investigation into the 1993 murder of my son Stephen made seventy recommendations. In 2021 – twenty-two years later – a parliamentary review found that while there had been 'significant improvements in the policing of racist crimes', there remain 'persistent, deep rooted and unjustified racial disparities'.[3]

One of the most striking such disparities may be observed in the use of 'stop and search' in London, whereby officers have the right to search someone if they have 'reasonable' grounds to believe that person is carrying something illegal, such as drugs or a weapon. Almost half of the total of all such procedures by Britain's forty-three police forces are carried out by the Met, and Black people and ethnic minorities are subjected to them almost nine times more frequently than white people.[4] The Met claim that this is a consequence of the higher concentration of Black, Asian and Minority Ethnic people in the population of London (40 per cent) than in that of the rest of England and Wales (10 per cent), but that does not explain the disproportionate number of shakedowns that Black Londoners currently endure. My inference is that the police of London presume that Black, Asian and Minority Ethnic people are more likely to be criminals than white people. This is racial profiling; racial profiling is an ethnic generalization; all ethnic generalizations are false.

An Avoidable Crisis, my 2020 report for the Labour Party leader Sir Keir Starmer on the impact of COVID-19, demonstrated that Black, Asian and Minority Ethnic communities were disproportionately and devastatingly impacted by the pandemic, and that they were victims of structural racism against which the Tory government had failed to take sufficient action. At about the same time, the murder of George Floyd by a racist policeman in Minneapolis, Minnesota, USA, brought the Black Lives Matter movement to prominence in Britain. The Tory government's response? Prime Minister Boris Johnson announced a Commission on Race and Ethnic Disparities. As Labour's shadow justice secretary David Lammy wrote in *The Guardian*: 'We do not need another review, or report, or commission [he named four such studies, including his own] to tell us what to do … It is time for action on the countless reviews, reports and commissions on race that have already been completed.'[5]

Johnson did no more than kick the can down the road. The spreading feeling that governments aren't doing enough to help people contributes to a general disaffection with the democratic process, and the reluctant conclusion that politicians come out only once in each electoral cycle to get our votes and, having got them, disregard us until the next time. Surely governments can be proactive without being interventionist? I think they used to be and hope they can be so again.

So my dreams for London in the twenty-second century are linked. I want a need-blind and colourblind city in which everyone who provides an essential service – in the public sector or the private sector – can afford to live near his or her place of work. I want people to understand their own and everyone else's backgrounds. I want politicians to say what they mean, mean what they say and be held to greater account for what they do and don't do. I want a city in which everyone can walk the streets day and night without let or hindrance either by criminals or by the people who are paid to keep us safe from them. And I believe that these dreams can and must come true.

Notes

1 'Three Million New Social Homes Key to Solving Housing Crisis', Shelter, 14 January 2019, https://england.shelter. org.uk/media/press_release/three_ million_new_social_homes_key_to_ solving_housing_crisis2.

2 See Hansard, vol. 662, 19 June 2019, https://hansard.parliament.uk/ Commons/2019-06-19/debates/ EC05E037-3BEF-4E2D-8642-1CC3A5D12397/PrimeMinister.

3 Home Affairs Committee, 'The Macpherson Report: Twenty-Two Years On', 30 July 2021, www.publications. parliament.uk/pa/cm5802/cmselect/ cmhaff/139/13903.htm.

4 Vikram Dodd, 'Black People Nine Times More Likely to Face Stop and Search than White People', *The Guardian*, 27 October 2020, www. theguardian.com/uk-news/2020/ oct/27/black-people-nine-times-more-likely-to-face-stop-and-search-than-white-people. See also Home Office, 'Police Powers and Procedures, England and Wales, year ending 31 March 2020, second edition', 27 October 2020, www.gov.uk/ government/statistics/police-powers-and-procedures-england-and-wales-year-ending-31-march-2020.

5 David Lammy, 'Britain Needs Leadership on Race Inequality. Not Just Another Review', *The Guardian*, 16 June 2020, www.theguardian.com/ commentisfree/2020/jun/16/race-inequality-review-boris-johnson-black-lives-matter-david-lammy.

Capital Growth

Tony Travers

The first issue to examine in any consideration of the future of London is whether the city's long history provides clues to its potential to survive large-scale, difficult events. Some major cities have declined from an apparently permanent position of international prominence in the past. There is certainly more competition for such places as London, Paris and New York today than there was in the early twentieth century. Megacities in South Asia, East Asia, Africa and Latin America have in many cases already exceeded London's population in size and, over time, will overtake European and North American cities' economic power.

London enjoyed a relatively long run of growth and economic success from the mid-1980s until the end of the 2010s. Having been affected by deindustrialization and population decline between the 1950s and 1980s, the capital experienced the return of relative and absolute expansion. The city became so apparently successful that the result of the Brexit referendum in 2016 was widely interpreted as being a demand for 'levelling up' between affluent London and an impoverished 'rest of the UK' (as well as for leaving the European Union). Perhaps inevitably, some policies put forward to achieve levelling up (such as the Arts Council's proposals to remove funding from English National Opera and require it to leave London) have risked 'levelling down' outcomes.[1]

The COVID-19 pandemic had a profound effect on cities, particularly within central business districts (CBDs). Because CBDs rely heavily on commuters, tourists and business visitors, the near-total absence of such people produced a far greater economic impact in these 'downtown' areas than in suburban areas. There were reports of people leaving many large cities for smaller towns or the countryside. Working from home during the pandemic appears to have produced a longer-term tendency for people to spend a smaller proportion of the week in offices and other workplaces.[2]

The future of London will thus include the possibility of a longer-term adjustment to different working and travel patterns. The agglomeration benefits of large cities may become less advantageous. Alternatively, high productivity might be achieved by a geographically extended version of London. Such potential outcomes will undoubtedly be researched in the decades ahead.

Many commentators have considered the pandemic in the context of earlier disasters to befall London, such as plague, the Great Fire of 1666, cholera epidemics, the Blitz during the Second World War, deindustrialization and the financial crisis of 2008. London recovered from such visitations, although not always immediately.[3] What we do know from the city's longer-term evolution is that the administrative boundaries and/ or the continuous urban area of London are never just the extent of its economy or influence. The concept of 'Greater London' had already existed for many years up to 1965 (when it became formally an administrative area established through the London Government Act of 1963), although with few effective government institutions to plan or represent it. Against this backdrop, the section on 'The future' (page 94) will attempt to assess the potential impact of the COVID-19 pandemic and other recent events, including the return of war in Europe after Russia's invasion of Ukraine in 2022, on London's long-term chances of success.

Growth and resilience

London's resilience since the year 1000 – when the city began to evolve into its modern form – cannot be doubted. There have been periods of decline as well as fast growth, but even the most challenging setbacks have proved only temporary. Population decrease and economic regression have

Looking eastwards along an empty Fleet Street, during an early COVID-19 lockdown.

occurred particularly after outbreaks of plague, war and fire, and during phases of rapid economic adjustment, such as the decline of the docks and industry from the 1960s to the 1980s. The measurement of 'growth' and 'decline' is made more difficult because the London of, say, 1300 is very different from today's metropolis.

The ancient city of London and its immediate surrounds (including Westminster, then separate) experienced periodic growth and shrinkage during the Middle Ages, but all within a relatively contained urban area that grew outwards only slowly. Then, as the city expanded more rapidly during the seventeenth and eighteenth centuries into what is today the West End, Southwark and Tower Hamlets, the very concept of 'London' changed. By the time railways (and later roads) had allowed further development to create a vast metropolis covering hundreds of square miles, the original City of London sat in the middle of a vast 'province of houses'.[4] Beyond the continuously built-up city lay the 'Home Counties': a patchwork of towns, suburbs and countryside that were, to varying degrees, linked to its economy and demographics. This area (extended to encompass East Anglia), including London, constitutes today's 'Greater Southeast' (GSE).

The outward sprawl of London, notwithstanding the imposition of a Green Belt, means that the administrative area covered by the Greater London Authority (GLA) is effectively an economic and demographic dynamo. It has a population of 9 million but lies at the centre of one of the world's largest 'city regions', the total population of which is 24 million.

London within the United Kingdom

This largely unplanned growth, and certainly the creation of a single dominant city, has had unintended consequences for the UK. Most obviously, 23 per cent of the country's economic output is produced in less than 1 per cent of its territory. If we look at the wider city region, 47 per cent of the UK's gross domestic product (GDP) is produced in 16 per cent of its land area.[5] Moreover, this concentration of national output is in the far southeastern corner of the country. It is hard to imagine such an outcome being deliberately pursued if it had not occurred by accident.

This process has been evolving for more than 150 years. The table below shows the estimated share of the UK's GDP of London, the GSE and the rest of the country in 1871, 1911 and 2020. London and the GSE have grown (in terms of GDP) relative to the UK as a whole between 1871 and 2020. There have been periods, notably between the 1940s and 1980s, when in relative terms London declined, but the GSE continued to expand.

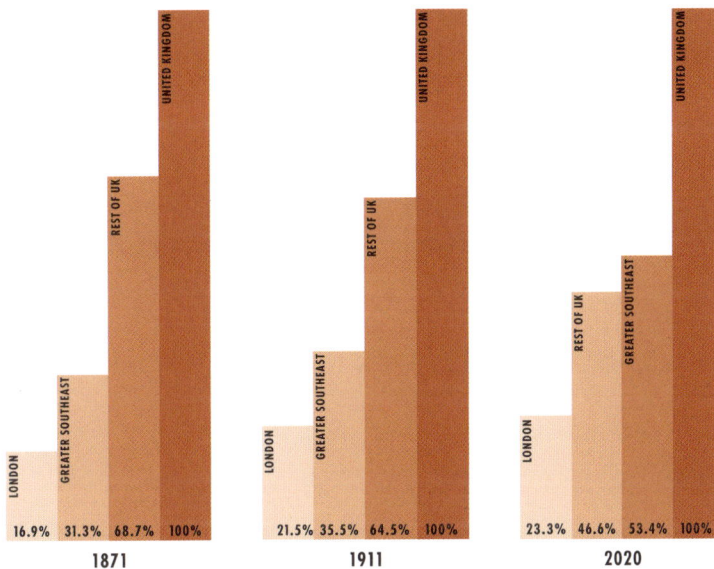

Regional GDP share of the United Kingdom.[6]

Historic forces have changed the economic geography of the UK over a protracted period.

London's outward growth between 1918 and 1939 created a megacity with a continuous urban area that is significantly larger than, say, that of Greater Manchester or the Birmingham/West Midlands city region. The population and economic importance of the ring of counties, towns and countryside surrounding London have continued to grow in the decades since 'Greater London' reached its current boundary.

Owing to this unplanned agglomeration, and to the large number of mostly uncoordinated local government units within both the continuously urban area of London and the partly urban southeastern and eastern regions of England, the GSE has become a flexible and economically successful city region. The area is close to, and has good links to, continental Europe. Three major airports ensure global connectivity, as do four major sea ports.

Many cities and towns surrounding London owe their economic power to the fact that they are close to the capital. Equally, London benefits from being, in effect, a significantly larger city than its administrative boundaries would suggest. Economic geographers have long recognized that the London economy involves a far wider area than the city itself. There is no regional government and thus little chance to plan growth or to constrain long-term population increase. There has therefore been an enduring tendency for the wider London region to grow relative to the rest of the UK.

Fifteen of the top twenty local authorities in the UK in terms of population growth between 2011 and 2021 are in the GSE, two are in the Southwest and two are in the South Midlands. Only one of the top twenty is in the three northern regions.[7] Unless government policies or economic change disrupt this long-term pattern, the GSE will eventually account for half of the UK's GDP, and half of the country's population. Since the 1950s the population of London itself (within the remit of the GLA) has increased more slowly than that of the ring of authorities surrounding the city, while the area beyond this inner boundary has grown even faster.

The future

For at least 150 years, housing construction and population have grown within the GSE. Moreover, the concentration of private-sector employment and activity in this region is even more pronounced. Public-sector employment as a proportion of all jobs is lower in London, the Southeast and the east of England than in other regions, whereas in Northern Ireland, Wales and Scotland the public sector is relatively more important.[8] Unsurprisingly, London and the Southeast have the largest number of businesses of any UK region and a high proportion of businesses relative to population size.[9]

There is no reason, under existing policies, to believe that the trends outlined here will change significantly in the coming decades. The government's 2022 Levelling Up White Paper put forward policies to assist localities that have relatively low GDP per head, lagging productivity and a poor quality of life.[10] Such proposals included the creation of free ports (special economic zones), grants to improve town centres, High Speed 2 (the new rail line from London to Manchester via Birmingham), regeneration of several city centres, and a commitment to direct a proportion of science and arts funding away from London and the Southeast. Later, new 'investment zones' were announced for locations across the UK.[11] But against the longer-term trends outlined earlier, these interventions appear modest.

An early analysis shows that possible economic and population trends set in train by COVID-19, Brexit and war in Europe are likely to be mildly negative for London, although probably no more so than for the UK as a whole.[12] The endgame of the Brexit process had demographic and economic impact. This is contested to the point at which a balanced judgement is virtually impossible, although over time figures for GDP per capita comparing the UK with other countries will make it easier to see what has really happened.

There is no robust and fully credible measure of how many people moved out of London in 2020 and 2021, but the population census undertaken during the spring of 2021 produced a figure for the city of about 200,000 fewer people than in the mid-year estimate for that year. Some of those who left will already have returned, while the trajectory of the city's population still appears to be upwards.

Working from home is another change that could affect London significantly, particularly its central area. The Office for National Statistics quarterly regional GDP figures suggest that London was not affected disproportionately by the pandemic.[13] By the autumn of 2022 it was clear that leisure travel was recovering more rapidly than commuting. Rising energy prices resulting from the Ukrainian war affect London and the

Working from home is not feasible for everyone who is required to do it, and as a result, demand for shared workspaces has increased.

Southeast less than other regions because, particularly in London, homes are smaller.[14] Also, the weather is generally warmer in the GSE than in northern regions, so less heating is required.

After the start of the pandemic, there was much media coverage of people 'selling up' and leaving London for other parts of the country.[15] At the time of writing Hamptons, a major estate agent, has a section of its website entitled 'Are you considering leaving London?', with elegant homes on offer in the counties surrounding London, plus Bristol.[16] According to the firm, first-time buyers in 2020 were moving on average 42 kilometres (26 miles) out of the capital, and those selling homes were moving about 64 kilometres (40 miles): 'This means the average person leaving London ... travels as far as Cambridge to the north, Colchester to the east, Brighton to the south or Didcot to the west.'[17] Although the pandemic increased the number of Londoners moving out of the city, this was rather less dramatic than headlines suggest. Moreover, the overwhelming majority of those leaving settled in the GSE. Homes sold in London by those moving out were not standing empty, suggesting a continued market in the capital.

For transport operators, such a trend would mean a shift from daily peak-hour commuting within the built-up London area to more irregular off-peak travel over longer distances across the GSE. For central London, it is likely that tourism, leisure and cultural activities will return to pre-2020 levels, but that office use will change. Occupiers will presumably shrink their office size to match the number of people at their desks over a 'smoothed' working week. Over time this will release office space for users who could not previously afford to operate in central London. The numbers of smaller office units and rent-by-the-day spaces are likely to increase further. But the final outcome of such responses to COVID-19 is still uncertain.

International inward migration has continued, although since 2020 (the end of the Brexit transition) there has been a significant shift from European Union (EU) to non-EU migration.[18] Non-EU migration has long been a source of population growth in London and other large cities in the UK. Combining the shift in outward migration as a result of the pandemic with Brexit-related changes in inward migration suggests that London will become a city with an even higher proportion of inhabitants who were born overseas. Migration trends in 2022 and 2023 suggest strong growth in non-EU migration to the EU and London.

It seems likely that London will see a return to population growth from 2022 onwards, following a modest dip in 2020–21. People moving out of London into the surrounding counties and districts will enhance the established trend for population and GDP growth in the GSE as a whole. There will probably be further increases in the number of people living in central London, although land constraints may limit growth unless there are major changes of building use. Attitudes to the need for open space and land availability will affect population growth in both inner and outer London. The dynamic relationship with the rest of the GSE is likely to remain as in previous decades.

Thus, it is possible that the pandemic and Brexit will boost the GSE's long-term growth by a mixture of internal dynamics and international inward movement of people. 'London' will have, in effect, spread out a little, but the relationship between the city and its region is likely to expand GDP in the medium term. The strength of the UK and GSE economy will, of course, influence net inward migration and the property market.

The relationship between London, the Greater Southeast and the rest of the United Kingdom

'Levelling up' and its politics between 2019 and 2022 created a negative dynamic within the UK. Because levelling up was often presented, particularly by some think-tanks, as an attack on London, the policy has become yet another element in a 'soft civil war' across the UK. Scottish Nationalism is often defined as 'against the UK government', while Brexit has created stress affecting Northern Ireland's position within the UK, kindling greater pressure for reunification with the Republic of Ireland.

Within England, relatively high public expenditure per capita in London is compared with that in the northern regions, while Scotland's (even higher) spending is not considered problematic. If public expenditure across the GSE is compared with that in other English regions (a fairer comparison because London, unlike any other UK nation or region, is virtually 100 per cent urban), regional spending differences are far smaller. But the dynamic that sets northern regions against London, which is not entirely new, appears to have been intensified by efforts to level up.

In fairness to lobbyists for different parts of the UK, the centralization of British politics invites an endless approach to resource distribution that involves spending money intended for one thing on another. Transport in the Northwest, Northeast, and Yorkshire and Humberside is indeed competing with London for government funding. More money for Leeds or Birmingham will mean less for London and vice versa, unless overall spending increases. City regional mayors and combined authorities in England have little freedom to raise taxes because the Treasury will not allow it. The autocratic seventeenth-century king Louis XIV of France would recognize with delight the centralized nature of the contemporary British State.

Although outside the scope of this essay, the extent to which parts of the UK must compete for resources and power appears increasingly destructive. Central government in Whitehall is too strong, yet too weak, to deliver services effectively and sensitively to a population in England of 56.5 million people.[19] The centre cannot realistically govern the whole country, whether from London or any other single point. The UK government is attempting to be both a nation-state like Germany and, at the same time, a vast district council. It is easy to blame 'London', as both a place and a shorthand for 'the government', for public service failures and economic woes.

Levelling-up policies pursued under the premiership of Boris Johnson (2019–22) encouraged interregional rivalries while not being powerful enough to deliver the kind of economic change that was promised. London, the Southeast and eastern England, even if neglected by national policymakers, are most likely to continue to prosper, albeit with lower levels of investment and, correspondingly, more stress.

Conclusion

Nothing is inevitable in politics, economics and government. But the long-term patterns explored in this essay suggest that London and its region are likely to continue to grow relative to the rest of the UK – and may even be encouraged to. Recent national and global events may affect the UK negatively (or positively), but there is no evidence at present to suggest a radical shift in regional economic and demographic outcomes across the UK. In the same way that earlier plagues, fires and wars did not push London into a permanent downward trajectory, the various 'once-in-a-lifetime' shocks that have occurred since 2008 also seem unlikely to. GDP figures published in the first half of 2023 showed London's economy continuing to grow faster than other parts of the UK in the early post-COVID period.[20]

A scenario in which London and the GSE extend their domination would raise new questions about the fragility of the UK and about London and the GSE's impact on national cohesion. Is London an economic benefit, or do the city and its region somehow threaten the rest of the country? Is a 'soft civil war', where nations and regions grow apart, a good or a bad thing? Such separation might encourage genuine devolution and a move to a constitutionally federal UK. But it might also lead to an increasingly miserable national argument, where rancour and envy prosper at the expense of subnational civic pride.

Paradoxically, in the massively centralized UK, only Westminster and Whitehall can initiate any move to devolution and national renewal. A problematic mixture of internal competition for Treasury-controlled resources, political rivalries between the UK government and the leaders of subnational areas, and policy drift at the centre threaten national cohesion. London will survive, but will the UK?

Notes

1 For an analysis of this challenge, see 'Levelling Up Agenda Risks Levelling Down London', in Patrick Diamond, Claire Harding and Farah Hussain, *East x South East: Local Research in Poplar, Stratford and Thamesmead*, Centre for London and Queen Mary, University of London, May 2022, www.qmul.ac.uk/mei/media/mei/tgc-media/filesx2fpublications/CfL_ExSE_QMUL_Report_Final.pdf.

2 See, for example, Alexander Jan, Nicolas Bosetti, Kieran Connelly and Jon Tabbush, *Global Cities Survey*, London Property Alliance, 2022, www.londonpropertyalliance.com/global-cities-survey.

3 See, for example, Neil Cummins, Morgan Kelly and Cormac Ó Gráda, 'Coronavirus from the Perspective of 17th Century Plague', 21 April 2020, www.cepr.org/voxeu/columns/coronavirus-perspective-17th-century-plague.

4 H.G. Wells, *The War of the Worlds* [1898] (1st World Library, 2003), p. 239.

5 Regional and National Economic Indicators, House of Commons Library, 2022, https://commonslibrary.parliament.uk/research-briefings/sn06924.

6 1871 and 1911 figures: Nicholas F.R. Crafts, 'Regional GDP in Britain 1871–1911: Some Estimates, Working Paper 03/04, Department of Economic History, London School of Economics, March 2004, http://eprints.lse.ac.uk/22557/1/0304Crafts.pdf; 2020 figures: 'Regional Economic Activity by Gross Domestic Product, UK: 1998 to 2020', Office for National Statistics, 2022, www.ons.gov.uk/economy/grossdomesticproductgdp/bulletins/regionaleconomicactivitybygrossdomesticproductuk/latest.

7 Callum May and Data Journalism Team, 'Census: Population of England and Wales Grew 6% in a Decade', *BBC News*, 28 June 2022, www.bbc.com/news/uk-61966084.

8 Niamh Foley, *Public Sector Employment by Parliamentary Constituency*, House of Commons Library, Briefing Paper no. 05635, 2 December 2020, https://researchbriefings.files.parliament.uk/

documents/SN05635/SN05635.pdf.

9 Federation of Small Businesses (FSB), *UK Small Business Statistics*, 2021, www.fsb.org.uk/uk-small-business-statistics.html; Department for Business, Energy and Industrial Strategy, *Business Population Estimates*, 2021, www.gov.uk/government/statistics/business-population-estimates-2021.

10 Department for Levelling Up, Housing and Communities, *Levelling Up the United Kingdom*, CP 604, 2022, www.gov.uk/government/publications/levelling-up-the-united-kingdom.

11 HM Treasury, *The Growth Plan*, CP 743, September 2022, https://assets.publishing.service.gov.uk/government/uploads/system/uploads/attachment_data/file/1105989/CCS207_CCS0822746402-001_SECURE_HMT_Autumn_Statement_2022_BOOK_Web_Accessible.pdf (see Investment Zones factsheet: www.gov.uk/government/publications/the-growth-plan-2022-factsheet-on-investment-zones/the-growth-plan-2022-investment-zones-factsheet; accessed 26 March 2023).

12 Office for Budget Responsibility, *Impact of the Brexit Trade Agreement on Our Economy Forecast*, March 2021, www.obr.uk/box/impact-of-the-brexit-trade-agreement-on-our-economy-forecast.

13 Office for National Statistics, 'GDP Monthly Estimate, UK: June 2022', www.ons.gov.uk/economy/grossdomesticproductgdp/bulletins/gdpmonthlyestimateuk/june2022.

14 Centre for Cities, *Cost of Living Tracker*, www.centreforcities.org/data/cost-of-living-tracker (accessed March 2023).

15 See, for example, Jack Sidders, 'Londoners Leaving the City in Droves as Covid Trend Persists', Bloomberg UK, 1 August 2022, www.bloomberg.com/news/articles/2022-07-31/londoners-leaving-the-city-in-droves-as-covid-trend-persists.

16 'Are You Considering Leaving London?', Hamptons estate agent, www.hamptons.co.uk/leaving-london (accessed March 2023).

17 'London Leavers Buy 73,950 Homes outside the Capital', Hamptons estate agent, December 2020, www.hamptons.co.uk/research/articles/london-leavers-buy-73950-homes-outside-the-capital-in-2020.

18 Office for National Statistics, 'Long-term International Migration, Provisional: Year Ending June 2021', 26 May 2022, www.ons.gov.uk/peoplepopulationandcommunity/populationandmigration/internationalmigration/bulletins/longterminternationalmigrationprovisional/june2021.

19 Office for National Statistics, 'Population and Household Estimates, England and Wales: Census 2021, Unrounded Data', 2 November 2022, www.ons.gov.uk/peoplepopulationandcommunity/populationandmigration/populationestimates/bulletins/populationandhouseholdestimatesenglandandwales/census2021unroundeddata.

20 Office for National Statistics, 'GDP: UK Regions and Countries: July to September 2022', 2023, www.ons.gov.uk/releases/gdpukregionsandcountriesjulytoseptember2022.

The new Palace of Westminster, seat of the UK Parliament, designed by Charles Barry with Augustus Welby Northmore Pugin, was completed in the 1870s after more than thirty years of construction.

London's New Nickname

Mark Stevenson

No one really knows when London got its new nickname. Some date it to a speech given by the Governor of the Bank of England at the UK Treasury in 2038, but it's clear the term was in common use before she made it the focus of her address. Others have suggested that it came from a talk by the CEO of one of the businesses at the centre of the new trade, as she explained why her company was floating on the London Stock Exchange and not in New York. Some pointed to an article in *The Economist*, others to a collection of essays gathered by The London Society (asking writers to imagine the city a hundred years in the future), published in 2023. Depressingly, but unsurprisingly, some opportunist politicians claimed they had coined it. The former prime minister Boris Johnson, shortly before his tragicomedic death, and with classic Johnsonian bluff, was adamant not only that he had come up with the term, but also that his leadership had been responsible for catalysing the whole industry. He was right in one way. After all, it was his government that was found by the UK High Court to be breaking its own net-zero law by failing to provide a credible climate plan for the nation – and this did indeed stimulate action.

Londoners in general started using the nickname when the architecture of their city began to change visibly, and it was in common parlance by 2050. By then nearly every large office block acted as a symbol of what London had become. The change in the buildings was initiated early in the 2030s, when an alliance of Architects Declare (a network of architectural practices committed to addressing the climate and biodiversity emergency), the CEOs of some of the biggest developers, several large property investment funds and a gaggle of 'celebrity' business leaders successfully lobbied the government finally to do something the construction industry had been asking it to do for decades – something both incredibly mundane and incredibly important – namely to change the rules on VAT for buildings. Previously, newly constructed buildings were not subject to VAT, while retrofits attracted the full rate of 20 per cent. A simple swap brought an end to the trend of destroying perfectly sound buildings in order to put up shiny new ones (with their attendant and eye-watering levels of embedded carbon), and the retrofitting boom started in earnest.

Another factor was that the First Pandemic (now regarded as benign compared to what came later in the 2020s) had brought a massive shift in working patterns. Employees, unwilling to give up the rights they had won during COVID-19, demanded the flexibility to work at home when they wanted to. Enlightened employers realized that this arrangement, if managed well, worked better for everyone and was considerably cheaper than maintaining expensive real estate (no matter the blandishments their landlords were increasingly forced to offer). As it was, offices were only 60 per cent occupied before the pandemic. Afterwards the occupancy rate never got above 40 per cent, which left a lot of space free – space that was costing its owners a pretty penny. This led over time to the City of London becoming a residential area once more, as empty offices (in part thanks to that VAT change) were retrofitted to become homes. Previously dead at the weekend, the City was now a bustling social and family centre as much as a business destination. And, if you looked up, you could see the other change. Floors of previously unused space were now being put to use combating the climate emergency and boosting the United Kingdom's economy at the same time.

Many argue that it was the British Council for Offices' new Code of Best Practice, published in 2033, that lit the touchpaper for this second change. From that point on, if you wanted to claim your office was of the highest specification, not only had it to adhere to the council's edicts on low-carbon retrofitting, but also it needed to remove carbon dioxide (CO_2)

from the sky. By 2040 a new wave of cheap-to-run, quiet direct air capture (DAC) modules had begun to fill the higher floors of the most prestigious blocks. Pipes directed the captured CO_2 to liquid storage facilities in the basement, where electric trucks would periodically come to take it to the mineralization facilities that were popping up all over the place. Pumped underground, the CO_2 formed a carbonate with rock, locking it away for all eternity. Instead of costing their owners money, these DAC floors were now earning them hard cash.

Since the early 2020s enlightened corporates had been paying to remove the carbon they were emitting, but slowly legislation tightened and what had been voluntary became a legal requirement. 'What goes up must now come down' was the strapline that accompanied the UK's 2031 Carbon Removal Act. It was a neat piece of law whose origins could be traced to the United Nations Climate Change Conference of the Parties (COP26) held in Glasgow ten years earlier, when the then Chancellor of the Exchequer Rishi Sunak announced that all UK firms over a certain size would now be legally required to publish a net-zero plan. Initially, those plans were full of holes, including the government's own – leading to the aforementioned legal defeat – but slowly they got better, with the result that every organization began to realize that it simply couldn't reach net zero without actually *removing* the emissions that it couldn't eradicate from its operations (and almost nobody could eradicate them all). The greenwash of 'offsetting' was soon exposed in the courts, thanks to a campaign led by such organizations as the Good Law Project and Client Earth (both in the team that had humbled Johnson's government), so durable and quick methods of carbon removal became an urgent need, stimulating an explosion of innovation – technically, financially and legislatively.

Now faced with the cost of cleaning up their own carbon mess, firms had a financial imperative to reduce their emissions earnestly and quickly, and the results were dramatic and swift. The UK's carbon footprint began to plummet. This rapid shift was made possible by a neat feature of the Carbon Removal Act that ensured UK-resident firms, in taking on their carbon debt, didn't sacrifice their competitiveness to foreign companies whose governments were lagging behind on the climate emergency. Firms that could demonstrate they were both cutting emissions and removing what was left were rewarded with reduced corporation tax on a sliding scale. With the best-performing firms (climate-wise) enjoying a delicious rate of 9 per cent (and, conversely, the worst offenders being asked for

A view of the City from the west is marred by a thick brown veil of pollution.

an eye-watering 50 per cent), London became the destination for the most climate-conscious (and almost by definition the most efficient and innovative) companies in the world, including all the leading providers of carbon removal that chose to headquarter themselves in the world's 'carbon capital'. The city's DAC floors were a proud badge of the new economy – and the economy was booming.

In 2022 the Intergovernmental Panel on Climate Change published its *Sixth Assessment Report*, describing the situation as 'Code Red for Humanity'. The report was clear. As well as radically cutting emissions, the world needed to remove roughly 200 billion tonnes of carbon from the atmosphere. London saw that if you created the right financial sticks and carrots to achieve that climate reality, it could become the centre for the biggest business opportunity in history.

Carbon removal at its peak would become a sector twice the size of that of oil and gas, retooling much of the talent that had built the fossil-fuel economy to remove the climate pollution it had created. Some commentators balked at this, but others pointed to the work, a century earlier, of one of the UK's most revered economists, John Maynard Keynes, who once suggested that a perfectly sensible way to boost a flagging economy was to pay people to dig holes in the ground and then to fill them up. The human race was doing much the same, just on a longer timescale than Keynes had imagined. It was perhaps fitting, therefore, that the Carbon Removal Act was championed by the UK Treasury, where Keynes had been an adviser.

The DAC floors were just one part of London's carbon-removal boom. All around the city other changes began to shape the built environment. Taking a leaf out of the regeneration of Detroit early in the twenty-first century, unused spaces became carbon-sequestering urban farms selling ultra-fresh produce to local restaurants. The Royal Borough of Greenwich, blessed with so much green space, became a major supplier of biochar (waste materials that are thermally decomposed rather than burned) to the capital, delighting gardeners with a carbon-fixing soil-amendment made from bio-waste cleared from its public parks. What new-builds were allowed were themselves stores of carbon, made from CO_2-fortified concrete or cross-laminated timber (so-called plyscrapers). The Ultra Low Emission Zone for vehicles, introduced in 2019, became the No Emission Zone twenty years later. But perhaps it was the rewilding of Soho, from 2052, that was the biggest symbol of what the city had now become, with businesses booming beneath the trees, and its swankier bars patronized by a newly rich class of carbon-traders and accountants.

And so London's old nickname 'The Smoke', associated with the fossil-fuel pollution that darkened its skies, was lost to memory and a new one became part and parcel of its modern identity. Today London, the financial centre of a new net-zero economy, is known around the world as 'Drawdown City', while Londoners simply call it 'The Sponge'.

The redeveloped Battersea Power Station – delayed by decades of prevarication and abandoned plans – is the focal point of the Vauxhall Nine Elms Battersea 'opportunity area'.

Big Capital
A City that Is 'Pre-something'

Anna Minton

'Surrounded by boxes yet again, about to move knowing that we will be moving again in the new year. I have cleaned and painted the flat and it's still a dump with damp patches and a moth eaten carpet throughout. I am forty-six and I have lived in over thirty houses and I still have no security ... In the adverts on the hoardings all over the city is another London, populated by smart-looking people and luxury balcony apartments. This is the destination of choice for foreign investors, and the new global elite of oligarchs, billionaires and the super-rich, who make up the so-called "alpha elites", who are attracted by the UK's very favourable tax environment. Entire neighbourhoods in the "alpha" parts of London – St John's Wood, Highgate, Hampstead, Notting Hill Gate, Kensington ... have changed out of all recognition in the last decade.'

This is the opening of my book *Big Capital* (2017), which makes the link between the growth of extreme wealth and the housing crisis. It was published two weeks before the Grenfell Tower fire that killed seventy-two people and was the most devastating residential fire in the UK since the Second World War. Several years later, London's extreme inequalities are even more pronounced and, despite the political instability that continues to follow Britain's exit from the European Union, London continues to attract the super-rich.

London's skyline has been transformed by one of the greatest waves of construction ever seen in the capital, with hundreds of new luxury residential towers. From Nine Elms up to Vauxhall and along to Southwark and Blackfriars bridges, along the south bank of the Thames, mile upon mile of apartments in gated complexes have been built. At Elephant and Castle the Australian property developer Lendlease is working with Southwark Council to render the area unrecognizable, replacing the affordable housing that once characterized it with a forest of gleaming towers. The £9 billion makeover of Battersea Power Station is at the pinnacle of this new London, where rooftop 'villas' are on the market for £8 million each, and shops include Rolex and Cartier, selling luxury watches and jewellery. Down the road in Nine Elms a 'Sky Pool' is suspended ten storeys up in the air between two high-end tower blocks.

There is a direct link between the wealth of those at the top and the capital's housing crisis, which affects not just those at the bottom but also the majority of Londoners, who cannot afford to buy homes or pay extortionate rents. The same currents of global capital are also transforming San Francisco, New York and Vancouver, European cities from Berlin to Barcelona, and cities and towns in the UK from Bristol and Manchester to Margate and Hastings. This isn't gentrification; it's another phenomenon entirely, driven by the sheer amount of capital that is being allowed to reconfigure the city.

Following the financial crash of 2008, the Bank of England, the Federal Reserve in the USA and the European Central Bank pursued a policy of quantitative easing (QE) to save the banks from collapse.[1] This continued in the UK until 2016, accelerating global housing inflation. Between 2009 and 2016 more than £445 billion was pumped into the economy. As a result of COVID-19 restrictions, this QE policy was repeated in 2020, resulting in the introduction of an additional £450 billion into the economy – more than in the seven years that followed the crash put together. And in 2022 the Bank of England's £65 billion intervention to buy government bonds to calm market panic was likened to a further round of QE. According to research from the Bank of England, the QE introduced after 2008 pushed up the price of a range of assets, in particular property, and was heavily skewed towards the wealthiest, with the top 5 per cent of households owning 40 per cent of these assets.[2] It is widely believed that the 2020 and 2022 tranches of QE are having a similarly inflationary impact on property prices.

House price inflation is the paradox that drives the British economy. It is both responsible for the lion's share of economic activity, measured by the increasingly discredited concept of Gross Domestic Product (GDP), and the reason why millions of people, particularly those under the age of fifty, are unable to buy their own homes.[3] The result is a situation where one part of the population is pitted against the other, with those who own gaining directly from the rising prices that exclude everyone else. And it explains the way in which stratospheric house price rises are still reported with jubilation, with breathless headlines boasting of the most expensive apartment ever, such as a flat at One Hyde Park in Knightsbridge, which sold for £111 million in 2021.[4] Another factor behind the politically ambivalent attitude to housing inflation is that house prices are left out of central banks' calculations on inflation. In the UK food, clothes, furniture and holidays are all included in the government's preferred inflation index, the Consumer Price Index, but house prices are not. Imagine, as inflation rises to politically unpalatable levels, if property prices were also part of those calculations?

Property inflation is not just something that affects those trying to get on to the housing ladder; it characterizes every aspect of housing, as not only property values but also rents rise throughout the city. The property consultant Savills has likened this to the 'champagne tower' effect, whereby 'billionaires displace multi-millionaires from the top addresses, so they in turn displace millionaires. Equity migrates to the more peripheral areas of the capital and, eventually, out of the capital to the rest of the UK.'[5] In London a combination of the super-rich, foreign investors and regeneration policies that favour the building of luxury apartment developments over affordable housing have created multiple displacement effects, which are mirrored in other cities. As communities are displaced from central London to suburban areas, property prices and rents go up in those places. The consequence is that average-income earners and the poor move to outlying areas or away from the capital altogether, to coastal towns, such as Hastings or Margate, or further afield, to Bristol or Cardiff, placing pressure on housing and prices in cities around the UK.

At the same time, a little-reported humanitarian crisis, condemned by the human-rights organization Amnesty International, is now unfolding in low-income housing in the UK. The acute shortage of social housing means that a third of social housing tenants (many of whom are on housing benefit) live in private rented housing, paying soaring rents that they cannot afford, facing choices between heating and eating, and enduring frequent evictions. This is a result of market policies replacing what would once have been the provision of council housing, in particular the interaction between 'right to buy' and 'buy to let', and the marketization of housing benefit. The Conservative prime minister Margaret Thatcher's defining policy of 'right to buy', instituted by the Housing Act (1980) and under which more than two million council homes have since been sold, continues to eat into the dwindling amount of genuinely affordable housing in England and Wales. As a result of that policy, 40 per cent of properties formerly owned by councils are now rented out by private landlords, at three to four times the price of social housing rents. According to government calculations, the local authority average social and affordable rent in England in 2020 was £343 per month, compared with £981 in the private sector.[6] In London the gap is even more stark, with social and affordable rents of £421 per month comparing with an average private-sector monthly rent of £1,603. The irony is that there is now such a shortage of social housing that local authorities themselves rent back thousands of former council homes, with boroughs across London spending £20 million in a single year renting back more than 2,300 properties at market rates.[7]

Inevitably, these soaring rents feed into a soaring housing benefit bill, running at £22 billion in 2019, around half of which sum is paid to private landlords. In an attempt to bring spending on housing benefit down, the government introduced in its place a complex market-based formula called Local Housing Allowance (LHA). Brought in at the tail end of the Labour government in 2008, LHA calculates an entitlement to subsidy for housing costs based on the lower levels of market rent in an area. From its introduction, it was clear that the amount of LHA often did not enable tenants to cover the rents they were paying. This became common after it was capped in 2011, and is now the norm. In London private renters face on average a gap of more than £200 a month, leading to a subsistence existence and frequent evictions when the rent goes unpaid. Although the cap was designed to bring the benefit bill down, rising rents have ensured the opposite has happened.

The human cost of the marketization of housing benefit is portrayed in the director Ken Loach's film *I, Daniel Blake*, in which the protagonist is forced to move from London to Newcastle. When the film came out in 2016 it was dismissed as 'a work of fiction' by the then government minister Greg Clark, but the story it tells, of councils routinely moving families out of London to cheaper areas as far afield as Slough, Maidenhead, Luton, Coventry and Glasgow, is now standard practice. Families have no choice but to accept housing far from home because if they refuse, they risk being labelled 'intentionally homeless' and therefore not eligible for social housing. The exporting of families out of London is fuelled by the market in benefit, because there are incentives for landlords in poorer parts of the country to work with councils in higher-value areas, since they receive more LHA than they would from local councils. But this in turn creates a housing shortage in those towns and cities, which then have to export their own residents to cheaper places, creating a domino effect across the country.

In 2012 the writer China Miéville said of a London 'buffeted by economic catastrophe' that 'This place is pre-something.'[8] More than a decade later it feels as though we know what that 'pre-something' was to become, as the city settled into its stratified and reconfigured patterns. 'Placemaking' took over every new district of the city, from Elephant and Castle and Greenwich Peninsula in the south to White City in the west, King's Cross in the north, and the Olympic Park and East Bank (a centre of arts, cultural and educational organizations) in the east. It's the same formula everywhere, with privatized enclaves of hundreds of unaffordable luxury apartments flanked by a high-end shopping centre, upscale restaurants and bars, and perhaps a university or museum. All these elements sit within a sterile, well-maintained and privately owned public realm, patrolled by security guards and closely monitored by closed-circuit television.

Within the city's public streets, with their stucco-fronted town houses built during the Georgian period, exclusion from the 'golden postcodes' of Hampstead and Highgate, Chelsea and Notting Hill is more covert than overt, but the effect is not dissimilar. Walking up Clarendon Road in Holland Park, where houses routinely sell for tens of millions of pounds, you can clearly see the outline of the devastated Grenfell Tower. The tragedy of the fire – described by a former chief fire officer as a 'Third World-type accident' – was brought about by failures directly linked to the idea of 'managed decline' that so often precedes the regeneration and 'placemaking' of an area.[9] Grenfell is in North Kensington, around the corner from some of the most expensive property in the world, and the culture that allowed residents' repeated concerns about safety to be ignored has to be seen in the context of decisions to regenerate the area.

The bigger picture is that all over London local communities are failing to benefit from the wholesale regeneration and reconfiguration of their areas. Entire districts are witnessing the demolition of estates that are replaced by ubiquitous developments of luxury apartments. In Elephant and Castle the Heygate Estate was demolished and replaced by Elephant Park, where two-bedroom apartments are on sale for more than £1 million each. Roughly 25 per cent of the scheme is designated as affordable housing, but the definition of that has been changed to mean up to 80 per cent of market value, so it is far from affordable for the majority of Londoners.

The refurbishment in 2016 of Grenfell Tower with flammable cladding (which was a fundamental cause of the fire) was also part of an area-wide regeneration, laid out in the 'Notting Barns Masterplan', which proposed creating 'a more successful urban neighbourhood through selective

The regeneration of redundant railway lands at King's Cross: a valuable new amenity, but for whom?

demolition of existing housing stock and the reprovision of high quality new homes'.[10] The aim was to drive up land values in the area by making it a more attractive place to live in, which is 'regeneration speak' for increasing property prices.

This is the new London and once again it is pre-something. What it is 'pre' to depends on how the city fares as the global and domestic economic picture darkens. With the likelihood that property prices will fall, one key player, the US private-equity giant Blackstone, is poised to play an ever larger role. The largest and most controversial landlord in the world, Blackstone already has a significant presence in the UK, having bought the 'railway arch' portfolio of England and Wales for £1.5 billion in 2019. This included more than 5,000 arches in gentrifying areas, underneath and alongside railway tracks that house small independent businesses, many of which were forced out by rent rises of more than 50 per cent. In 2020 Blackstone moved into student housing, with the £4.7 billion purchase of the student accommodation firm iQ reported to be the largest ever real-estate deal in the UK. At the time of writing, the cheapest student room listed on the iQ website as available in Bloomsbury, where many of London University's colleges are, was £493 per week for an 'entry-level' room of 13 square metres (140 square feet). Providing a context for the company's strategy of buying undervalued assets, CEO Steve Schwarzman, a close friend of the former US President Donald Trump, described it as 'basically waiting to see how beaten up people's psyches get, and where they're willing to sell assets … You want to wait until there's really blood in the streets.'[11] As property prices fall, Blackstone, which in October 2022 announced plans to expand its headquarters in Mayfair, is poised to clean up.

With recession looming, London's inequalities look set to grow ever starker, and optimism is in short supply. As consumers tighten their belts, the upscale privatized plazas that define the contemporary city are likely to be ever quieter, frequented only by a small swathe of wealthy customers. At the same time, austerity removes people on lower incomes from the capital altogether, clearing the city of the diverse and contested interests that characterize it, and creating sterile, hollowed-out enclaves in their place; gentrification has made way for sterilization. The French philosopher Henri Lefebvre described space as a 'social product' that cannot be 'removed from ideology and politics'.[12] These are the spaces and places that reflect our politics and our times.

Notes

1 Bank of England, 'Quantitative Easing', 31 January 2023, www.bankofengland. co.uk/monetary-policy/quantitative-easing.

2 Michael A.S. Joyce, Nick McLaren and Chris Young, 'Quantitative Easing in the United Kingdom: Evidence from Financial Markets on QE1 and QE2', *Oxford Review of Economic Policy*, XXVIII/4 (Winter 2012), pp. 671–701.

3 GDP does not account for huge wealth inequalities. Having been introduced during the manufacturing era, it deals only in economic transactions, so unpaid care and domestic work count for nothing, as do well-being and mental health.

4 Ruth Bloomfield, 'Penthouse in One Hyde Park Where Kylie Minogue Owns a Flat Sells for £111 Million', *Evening Standard*, 9 October 2021, www.standard.co.uk/homesandproperty/property-news/kylie-minogue-penthouse-sold-one-hyde-park-london-111m-b958921.html.

5 Quoted in Jon McDermott, 'The London Syndrome', *Prospect*, 14 November 2013, www.prospectmagazine.co.uk/magazine/the-london-syndrome-property-capital.

6 'Live Tables on Rents, Lettings and Tenancies', Gov.uk, 16 February 2023, www.gov.uk/government/statistical-data-sets/live-tables-on-rents-lettings-and-tenancies.

7 Tom Copley, 'Right to Buy: Wrong for London', January 2019, p. 7, www.london.gov.uk/sites/default/files/rtb_report_feb_update.pdf.

8 China Miéville, *London's Overthrow* (Westbourne Press, 2012), n.p.

9 Jon Hall, quoted in Martin Robinson, '"No Sprinklers or Fire Alarm" and Residents Told to Stay Inside: Tower Block's "Third World" Safety Failures', *Daily Mail*, 14 June 2017, www.dailymail.co.uk/news/article-4602436/No-sprinklers-fire-alarm-residents-stay-inside.html.

10 Royal Borough of Kensington and Chelsea, 'Notting Barns South: Draft Final Masterplan Report', July 2009, available at www.rbkc.gov.uk.

11 'Blackstone: Millions on the Line and Out for Blood', *Irish Independent*, 13 August 2014, www.independent.ie/business/irish/blackstone-billions-on-the-line-and-out-for-blood-30507450.html.

12 Henri Lefebvre, *The Production of Space* (Wiley, 1992).

The varied gardens on the roof of Goodman's Fields, Aldgate, offer a tantalizing glimpse of a greener city.

Moving Towards a Regenerative London

Sarah Ichioka

Flourish, the book I wrote in 2021 with the regenerative architect Michael Pawlyn, was created as an attempt to find our place as humans approach an existential turning point. This might sound melodramatic, but the moment provides us all with an opportunity to think about what we can contribute to the wider efforts to save humanity from extinction and the rest of life on Earth from the worst of our impacts. Michael and I have most influence within the built environment and the professions associated with it. Many of our peers are focusing on battles concerning regulations, codes and standards, all of which are very important, but this is not necessarily a way to bring about the wholesale systemic change that is so desperately needed.

Everything about the way in which humans live will need to change, which means re-examining how we conceive, design, build and manage our cities, particularly in the more heavily industrialized, wealthy world. The COVID-19 pandemic afforded us the opportunity to pause, research and rethink many of the processes that go into the creation and maintenance of buildings and spaces. By spending time with great thinkers beyond the field of architecture, we can locate relevant and visionary means of reframing the way in which our societies currently function. We thought that this was really important to bring into built-environment discourse, so *Flourish* is based on this premise of what is needed for humanity's survival and, hopefully, the ways in which it can thrive. At a fundamental level this means rethinking the mindsets that shape our collective behaviour. We set out our proposals as five main paradigms to help develop a regenerative future: Possibilism, Co-evolution as Nature, A Longer Now, Symbiogenesis and Planetary Health.

Learning from London's past

The current challenges facing London – in terms of political will, economic pressures and climatic shifts – are daunting but not insurmountable. In fact, the United Kingdom is one of the countries that has some of the more positive longer-term outlooks under conditions of planetary emergency. There are geographic advantages to its location within the northern hemisphere, as well as its material advantages, which have been partly built on the spoils of empire and are not something that should be celebrated.

The British Isles also have a long history of continuous habitation: the land has been adapted and repurposed many times to suit the changing needs of the population. London has been so many versions of itself, and you can easily read the different layers that make up these alterations, charting the ways in which it has grown and declined across the centuries. However, by studying London's past we realize that its resilience is based not just on its relative geographic security and geopolitical advantage but also on the strength of a socio-cultural history of reinvention. This is potentially a key source of positive impetus for us to consider. Sometimes it is necessary to take the longer view, so that we can understand how radical change is possible while at the same time how cities such as London can retain many of the key elements that define them. There doesn't seem to be a huge amount of confidence that the required change is coming at a national level but there are reasons for optimism at the scale of cities. The philosopher Roman Krznaric points out that cities are one of the oldest human technologies, and so perhaps they contain more room for hope of reinvention.[1]

Waste and the growth economy

Can London continue to take an insular view of the big challenges it faces, such as the huge amount of destruction and waste produced by the built environment industries? This is predicated on an endless cycle of creating new buildings to sell and lease. It's harder to lease properties in a competitive economy if they do not fit into an idealized vision of the new that satisfies the market. To answer this question, it would be helpful to look more closely at the City of London, which acts as the economic engine for the capital as a global city. At the highest level we need to consider the ultimate purpose of our cities and their financial systems. We must move away from the growth-at-all-costs mindset to which most businesses in London still seem to subscribe. We need to adopt an approach that is focused on planetary health as the lodestar of our economies. What would the City of London look like if all the institutions, businesses and individuals operating there moved away from the singular pursuit of growth to much more qualitative metrics that are based on understanding how our economy nests within natural systems?

Across the rest of the capital we see this constant cycle of take, make and waste. The mega-renovations of houses in places such as Chelsea have become the prime examples of this concept: vast basements are excavated, causing huge problems for the local area. This desire to improve properties' status and increase their value has met with public disdain and is at odds with the needs of the broader population. These worst caricatures must be rethought as we advocate for circularity in the built environment.

It is apparent that much of the waste produced by London's buildings is generated by the private sector, whether it's the headquarters for multinational companies or an oligarch's mansion. If we are fundamentally trying to get our priorities right, we should be focusing instead on a clear analysis of the amount of embodied carbon that we can afford to use. This means prioritizing the type of infrastructure that the writer George Monbiot calls 'public luxury', instead of the current model that is focused mainly on private sufficiency.[2] How can our budgets and material investments be reallocated to support the health of ecosystems, including the majority of people within them?

Natural solutions

Nature actually provides the answer to this question. There is no waste in nature; the outputs from one living creature become the inputs for another. We need to inspire future designers and like-minded individuals to find ways in which we can join up all our industries so that we minimize

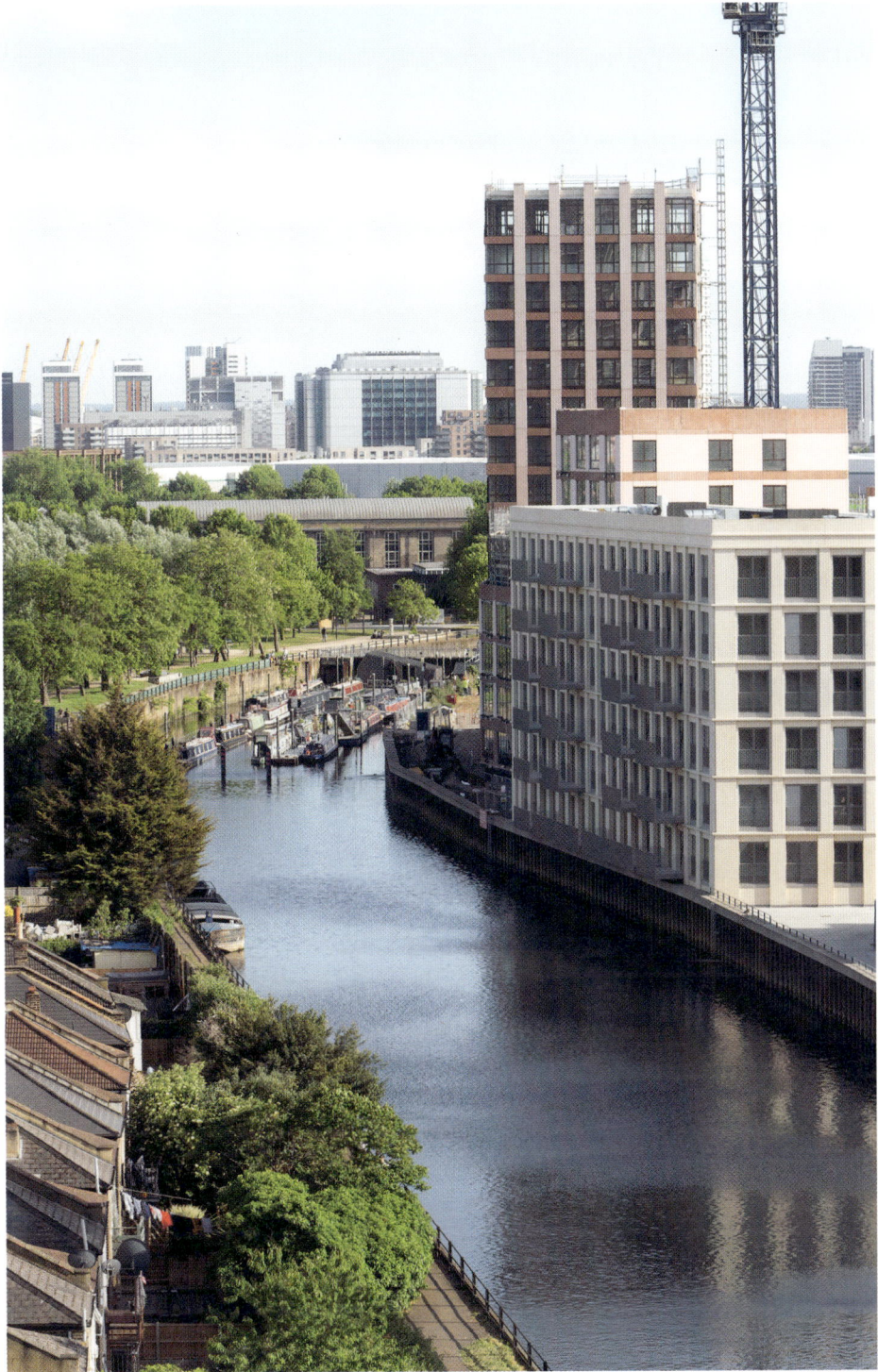

Three Mills Wall River Weir beside Sugar House Island in east London: an example of a public luxury – greening waterways – that is increasingly appreciated by city dwellers.

waste, and then completely rethink how it can be repurposed. There are promising examples of this process happening already: the UK has a surprising number of forward-thinking architects who are looking at ways to repurpose materials and make the best of renovating existing buildings, which contain most of the embodied carbon. And there are great campaigns such as RetroFirst, run by the *Architects' Journal*, which advocates for renovation as the first option.

If we accept that nature has proven that waste is actually a resource, then maybe there are some other things that we can learn about transforming our construction industry. In general, we humans tend to assemble our materials from high-energy bonds, which make them very difficult to recycle. Biology, on the other hand, has evolved to use low-energy materials that are easy to dismantle at standard temperatures and pressures, with 96 per cent of all living matter made from just four elements – carbon, hydrogen, oxygen and nitrogen – and the remaining 4 per cent from about seven additional elements. Right now human industry employs a much broader range of the periodic table, including more than 100 elements. This is further evidence that, with a fundamental rethink, natural systems could really help us find the answers we desperately need. Space could be found in parts of London where we can create eco-industrial parks for the collocation of different industries in a way that eliminates waste and connects cycles.

Changing climate

As global temperatures rise, London is getting hotter and wetter. We can make the city more resilient in two ways. First, we can use the wisdom shared by the biomimicry expert Janine Benyus, who always starts a project by asking what solutions already exist in this place. And that means both natural and cultural solutions. Luckily, London has many experts and design teams who understand natural systems fundamentally, from the earliest conception of a project through to its final execution. For instance, an intimate and specific understanding of hydrology and ecology will be a very helpful way of building more resilient parts of the city located, for example, in the middle of a floodplain. Our ancestors would never have built in these areas, but we now have the ability to modify existing human-made infrastructure so that it is more generously (and prudently) integrated within its landscape.

Another key inspiration comes from the philosopher Freya Matthews, who asks: 'What does nature want us to want?' Green and blue infrastructure are already fantastically popular, so how can we design even more greenery and access to water into London's urban fabric? We need to take that idea a step further to understand, for example: what does this underground tributary want us to want? When we're redesigning the street, how does it want to be daylighted? Does it want to have permeable surfaces so that it can recharge the water table? What do the ecosystems of our existing parks and green spaces want us to want? Do they want to be linked up to support migratory routes? What suits the needs of birds, mammals or insects living in London's existing green spaces? How do they like to travel? What do they need to have robust, flourishing and healthy ecological interaction throughout their whole life cycle? What sort of plants do pollinators want us to put on our rooftops and balconies? I think that opens up a whole new potential for creativity that is really exciting, but it requires new skillsets for designers or a generous ability to bring in collaborators who already have that knowledge.

The social component is an important way to approach the creation of a resilient London, which loops back to the idea of prioritizing investment in public luxury over private luxury. London does have many wonderful places of public luxury – among them Hyde Park, the Southbank Centre, the Natural History Museum and Hampstead Heath – but there is also a huge amount of funding going into the private sector. This helps us to think about which systems the city puts in place to support all its residents. We need to ascertain the level of social infrastructure that can create ties between neighbours so that they can be mutually supportive rather than competitive. Which sort of zoning policies will facilitate mixed-income neighbourhoods and avoid the 'gated community' mentality? Fundamentally, we have to improve the urban fabric to make life better for people, and it's been proven time and time again that access to nature is key for a better quality of life. Therefore, investing in what is good for other species is also, on the whole, better for our own mental and physical well-being.

Time and politics

Which time cycles or horizons should our economies and politics be run on? A corporation runs on quarterly performance reports. A trader on the London Stock Exchange thinks in terms of the daily cycle of the market, with some transactions happening in milliseconds. Politics is slower – ranging from two to four years, depending on the electoral cycle – but we're still seeing important decisions made based on short-term thinking despite the long-term significant repercussions they might have. Walking around London and experiencing the vestiges of previous generations and institutions, which hold the potential to be reinvented for today, can add a useful long-term perspective. It is not acceptable to think in terms of the binary opposition of preservation at all cost or tearing down and building anew. Instead, we have to think about ways in which we can reinvent an existing building or structure, which is probably also true of institutions. What would regenerative transformation look like, both in terms of the physical space and how it is inhabited or programmed?

There are key questions about governance and how we can create systems that act as a counterweight to the standard economic and political short-termist cycles of decision-making. The metropolitan level of governance actually holds the key for organizing such big changes over the coming decades. Seoul in South Korea offers a great example, as there was a dramatic shift within a few years at the turn of the millennium from a technocratic, insulated form of top-down city-planning to the current process, which is structured to be actively inclusive. Such change is possible in the metropolitan context because you can move towards ever more localized consultation, depending on the level of policy under discussion. It is then possible for the government to work directly with civil society to achieve shared goals.

Any programme that is going to transition to a truly green and just economy is key. We must move beyond ideas such as selling corporates carbon credits to enrich just 0.1 per cent of people. Fundamentally, regenerative development is about creating the right livelihoods for a broad spectrum of citizens. This is absolutely the right thing to do ethically and is important politically.

Bringing about the change

Everyone has a role to play in the transformation of London and the rest of the world. That can feel daunting when you consider the sheer scale of the change that needs to happen to decarbonize our economy and move towards a life-centric model. But, on the other hand, there are so many amazing organizations, networks, educational institutions, books and websites already developing and proposing viable solutions, so we are not starting from scratch by any means.

We need to build and add to that groundswell and find our particular place in it. I take a lot of inspiration from positive examples of this movement around the world, and there is genuinely strength in numbers. Industry standards are not going to shift until there is a signal, at least from a significant minority of people, who are willing to hold one another – and those at the top – accountable. That's why coalitions of companies, such as the Architects Climate Action Network and Built Environment Declares (Michael Pawlyn was a co-initiator of the latter group) are significant. I think it's fantastic that many British local authorities have their own movements too (such as Local Authorities Declare Climate and Biodiversity Emergency). If all those different chapters could join together – from local planners to interior designers and those working in the construction industry, for example – that collective impact will be strengthened. Eventually, what seemed unthinkable will just become the norm, the standard baseline for doing things, and that will shift world views through action. I've always loved the poet Antonio Machado's phrase *se hace camino al andar* (to make the road by walking).[3] In London, and around the planet, we have to walk together to create new paths, away from climate breakdown, towards a regenerative future.

Notes

1 Roman Krznaric, *The Good Ancestor: How to Think Long Term in a Short-Term World* (W.H. Allen, 2020), n.p.

2 George Monbiot, 'Public Luxury for All or Private Luxury for Some: This Is the Choice We Face', *The Guardian*, 31 May 2017, www.theguardian.com/commentisfree/2017/may/31/private-wealth-labour-common-space.

3 Antonio Machado (1875–1939), 'Caminante no hay camino', available in English as '[Traveler, your footprints]' in *There Is No Road* (White Pine Press, 2003).

The Future of Heritage
Conservation v2

Gillian Darley

Now that the Pluralist Society is the new name for the Twentieth Century Society, and all requests for listing buildings of special architectural and historic interest must be accompanied by a viable business and sustainability plan, the heritage sector has had to work much harder. Consider Harrods, the lavish old department store, which closed its doors to shoppers in the year of King Charles III's coronation. The repurposed palatial terracotta building, which stretches a full block and more, with a web of tunnels far below the Knightsbridge pavements, has proved to be an incredible success – in its guise as a deluxe health facility. The splendid 1890s retail emporium had been waiting for such a transformation.

Relax. My Baz Luhrmann-esque evocation is a flight of fancy, but not that far-fetched in a part of London in which untold wealth knows few limits. The essayists in the original *London of the Future* were considering the 'continuous evolution of a great city', much as we have been asked to do here.[1] Nothing was out of bounds. For them, economic success could, and must, coexist with 'beauty and dignity'.[2] Progress, fast and furious in the aftermath of war, suggested multiple threats to historic buildings, still then essentially unprotected by the law. For that reason The London Society – as its founding chairman, the leading architect Sir Aston Webb, wrote – would pledge itself

Bush House (1925) on Aldwych, designed by Harvey Wiley Corbett and used by the BBC from 1940 until 2012.

to 'the jealous preservation of all that is old and beautiful in London as far as is possible'.[3] Prosperity must not '[sweep] away any parts of old London'.[4]

Contributors to the original publication were eager to lay better foundations, urgently planning for a different world, a different kind of city. But they showed their age and their distance from the subsequent modern era. Lord Crewe (Robert Crewe-Milnes, 1st Marquess of Crewe) cited the value of 'the residences of great men' – oddly citing the quite modest homes of the writers Thomas Carlyle and Samuel Johnson – or masterpieces such as Richard Norman Shaw's New Scotland Yard.[5] Crewe had been (briefly) the chairman of the London County Council (LCC) and gave due credit to the wisdom of Laurence Gomme, clerk to the LCC and a co-author of two early volumes of the *Survey of London*. The latter was a statistician, the former a well-read Liberal politician, and in their words, like those of other contributors, we can sense the push and pull between the capital as it existed in 1921 and a London prepared for transformation in the economic interests of the country. Something had to give.

As the historian Andrew Saint writes, Gomme was 'a believer in the practical lessons of history'.[6] He ensured, for instance, that the buildings standing in the way of new roads, such as Holborn Kingsway and Aldwych, were carefully recorded before contractors scythed through the chaotic but often valuable historic fabric, much as the railways had earlier. Bush House, standing proud and new at the junction of those two roads, epitomized the coming imperatives and has, due to its site and stately architectural quality, survived to tell a worthwhile story. Named after and funded by the American mega-industrialist Irving T. Bush, it was designed as an international trade centre and opened in 1925. High above the entrance are two freestanding sculpted figures, their hands meeting on the base of a flaming torch above the inscription: 'To the friendship of English speaking peoples'.

After Second World War damage to Broadcasting House, when the British Broadcasting Corporation (BBC) required extensive premises, particularly for overseas broadcasts, it lit upon Bush House. The heroic central block and colonnades were listed Grade II in 1976, and the building remained the BBC World Service headquarters until 2012. After that, King's College London incorporated the authoritative, renovated building into its Aldwych campus, and in 2017 Bush House became King's Business School. The wheel of commerce and culture had come virtually full circle.

Now conservation is on the move, shifting direction, emphasis and purpose by the minute. Interestingly, even the blanket retention of existing buildings, including a 'blue sky' suggestion for a universal Grade III listing, rather like the proposal for a countrywide National Park, is an idea gaining a following.[7]

A listed building is a protected building, at least in theory. For that reason, five-year certificates of immunity (COIs) from listing are highly sought-after by developers or landowners. With that, buildings judged suitable for major change or even demolition, regardless of how powerful the arguments on their behalf and eloquent their advocates are, can find themselves scarily unprotected. There's been no clear explanation (despite plenty of conspiracy theories) why the Southbank Centre, that gritty cultural cluster consisting of the Hayward Gallery, the Queen Elizabeth Hall and the Purcell Room, found that its COI was renewed for the *fourth* time in 2018, as the government's Department for Digital, Culture, Media and Sport (DCMS; now the Department for Culture, Media and Sport) overturned the advice of Historic England, the advisory body on the historic environment, yet again. Sometimes (for better and for worse) these things hinge on something as transitory and subjective as the taste of an individual minister for or against unadorned concrete, but on other occasions an unseen string puller or interloper lurks in the wings.

In this case, as the certificate runs its course during 2023, it's plain that a far greater popular appetite for Brutalism, and appreciation of an exceptional modern exhibition space and the pleasant, low-key concert halls nearby, may make the Southbank Centre less easy to omit from listing. When the complex opened in 1967 it had a niche architectural audience, but recently, enhanced by major work on and around the Royal Festival Hall (long luxuriating in its Grade I designation and the pull of its origins in the 1951 Festival of Britain), it has gone mainstream, nay fashionable. As built heritage ages, taste changes, and in London at least, architectural conservation is being propelled ever faster into the future.

The thirty-year rule – the earliest moment at which a building in England or Wales can be designated for listing is when it is thirty years old – means that most of the new architecture I wrote about in my early days as a journalist in the professional and broadsheet press is either listed or long gone. In 1990 *The Observer* newspaper was based in Marco Polo House in Battersea; I felt ashamed to be covering architecture from such a crass building. I wished it gone (it proved a terrible workspace) but it wasn't demolished until 2014, not before moves were made to list it as an outlier of Post-modern architecture.

The organizations that drove (and still drive) the conservation world in the UK have their own anniversaries to celebrate. Grandparent of them all, the Society for the Protection of Ancient Buildings (SPAB), was set up by William Morris and the architect Philip Webb in 1877 in the face of heavy-handed restoration and falsification of old fabric. It initiated and continues the urgent task of training generations of building professionals and craftspeople, and inspiring a wider public. As Morris put it, 'We are only trustees for those who come after us.'[8] The dynamic organization SAVE Britain's Heritage, which began life by pumping out a press release a week during European Architectural Heritage Year (1975), still leads the campaigning pack, running neck and neck with the Twentieth Century Society (which, jesting apart, must soon alter its name). Innumerable bodies, special pleaders for typologies of buildings, for periods and styles, are proliferating in their wake.

The means by which news of a threat or bad decision is conveyed can be lightning fast – and is getting faster. Social media has proved a good friend of heritage. At best it spreads the word, speeds up campaigns, enlightens and informs. Consider the old days. The demise of the Firestone

The demolition of the Firestone Building, Brentford, 23 August 1980.

Building in Brentford at the hands of developer Trafalgar House occurred over a late summer bank holiday weekend at the very moment when the advice to list it had landed in the secretary of state's in-tray.

By coincidence, I was photographing it for a book about the delights of outer London. I stood on the central reservation of the Great West Road, also known as the 'Golden Mile' due to its rich crop of Art Deco factories, largely American firms serving the motor industry. The relative lack of traffic on a public holiday was as helpful to the demolition crews as it was to me. Uninterruptedly, balls swinging on chains were systematically shattering the outstanding feature of the front elevation, a wealth of coloured ceramic detail. I tried to photograph what I could from across the road and ran to a phone box, my films in hand. Feeding in coins frantically, I rang the *Sunday Times* for whom I occasionally worked. 'Oh no,' said the woman on the switchboard. 'Too late, the paper's gone to bed.' It was 4.30 pm, and centuries ago.

My memory is a kind of draughtboard of what went, what stayed, or even what was not to be. There was no more gripping saga than the developer Peter Palumbo's dogged desire for a towering office block designed by Ludwig Mies van der Rohe in Mansion House Square. Even if the tower in question was a somewhat jaded modernist reissue, the fight went to the wire. Tenacious Lord Palumbo did get a notable building, but it was to be the ingenious wedge-shaped Post-modern block designed by James Stirling. Listed since 2016, to see off proposed alterations, No. 1 Poultry offers a kind of cheeky prow, a vessel heading into the choppy waters of the City of London. It was completed five years after its architect's death. By then, few except the die-hards remembered the quaint, busy little row of commercial premises and chambers that Palumbo demolished, and that had provoked the argument in the first place. The complexities and contradictions, the switchbacks and new concerns that are knotted around contemporary cases would have dizzied the original members of The London Society, wedded to their near-certainties about what must go and what must stay, what counted and what was of no consequence.

As the decades pass, the listings jungle becomes ever denser. At one extreme is the gloriously extrovert Lloyd's Building (with its weird transplanted Georgian boardroom within) – which received a Grade I listing at the very edge of the time limit for such protection – and, at the other, Conservation Areas (introduced from 1967 onwards), which argue for overall character and sustaining the general scene, rather than the particular and the outstanding.

Where the financial stakes are highest, as in the City of London, the freedom to develop – and then redevelop – is fiercely guarded. Only one third of the City area is designated within Conservation Areas, but ways emerged to circumvent that irritating restriction. Across London, and particularly where land values are highest, stupendous and hugely costly engineering work has produced a series of Potemkin villages, mere façades behind which anything goes. What began as a trickle is now a flood, while submitted applications waffle about 'sense of place', 'context' and buildings 'in keeping' to placate planners and their almost-extinct colleagues, conservation officers. The weasel words may change but pressures mount inexorably along with property values.

The future of heritage is, inevitably, bound to be cyclical, and its fortunes dictated by anything from world events to local politics. Much of the shape of the capital is dictated from a distance, with speculative funders often on the other side of the world – or operating entirely out of sight. Battersea Power Station has a new mixed-use life (its chimneys all new) thanks to a Malaysian conglomerate. Compare that to the battle for Covent Garden market in the 1970s, an impassioned affair in which, eventually, the Greater London Council and a benevolent Conservative minister (Geoffrey Rippon) saw sense. Thirty or so years on, at King's Cross, the well-calibrated cross-fertilization between muscular retained and adapted warehouses, sophisticated landscape design and strong new architecture has worked well – even with the sceptics.

But what of a future forged in straitened economic circumstances? The first moves against a pig-headed Liverpool Street station development by the developers of the Shard, including Network Rail, have been a flurry of listings. The successfully upgraded 1980s station thoroughfare and canopies needed protection, while the Great Eastern Hotel deserved upgraded listing. The architects Herzog & de Meuron have proposed a crude airship full of offices, shops and a replacement hotel floating high above the station roofs. Those of us with long memories can recall that dreaded old chestnut, the exploitation of air rights for lucrative development, as rolled out in Manhattan in the 1970s. Here we go again.

Now fleet-footed, savvy conservation players must learn new skills. The store of unused buildings, starting on the high street and spilling out to the furthest limits of London, offers innumerable opportunities for conversion and repurposing, whether for NGOs (non-governmental organizations) or social enterprises, smart new businesses or refocused old ones. Something is stirring. Even if a building is unlisted, as in the case of the Marks & Spencer store on Oxford Street, which SAVE made a *cause célèbre* by fighting against its wasteful demolition at a public inquiry, there are persuasive, if complex, arguments in play.

These touch on every aspect of our attitude to the immediate future as they do to our recent past. Ideas need to be inverted, comparisons made, certainties queried. Future heritage will hinge on taking stock, evaluating, while carefully testing what is, and is not, viable. Looking ahead, listed buildings and Conservation Areas offer no more than brief breathing spaces and a little more time in which to prepare for action. The future is, in many ways, a question of looking backwards hard and quizzically.

Heritage specialists, from Historic England to the full range of amenity societies and pressure groups, with their professional advisers standing by, are becoming more informed and materially intelligent, learning innovative ways. It is a wide canvas, too. Conservation policy applied to public housing – even enormous, ageing schemes such as Arnold Circus in Bethnal Green, Churchill Gardens in Pimlico or Alexandra Road in Camden – makes it clear that listed heritage is not simply the stuff of esoteric or academic special interest but also socially and politically embedded.

The future of heritage in London is, put simply, effectively the future of London. Conservation ideals must meet construction standards while construction confronts environmental sustainability in all its dizzying complexity. These are urgent times, and surviving buildings – a resource of great value – must adapt or be gone. And, don't forget, what takes their place may well become another tranche of heritage.

Notes

1 *London of the Future* (E.P. Dutton & Co., 1921), p. 37.
2 Ibid.
3 Ibid., p. 16.
4 Ibid.
5 Ibid., pp. 274–6.
6 Andrew Saint, *London 1870–1914: A City at Its Zenith* (Lund Humphries, 2021), p. 210.
7 Will Arnold, 'Could a Grade III Listing for Buildings Halt the UK's Tide of Demolition?', *Architects' Journal*, 22 November 2022, www.architectsjournal.co.uk/news/opinion/could-a-grade-iii-listing-for-buildings-halt-the-uks-tide-of-demolition.
8 William Morris during an address given at the 12th Annual Meeting of the Society for the Preservation of Ancient Buildings, 1889. *Collected Works of William Morris* (Longmans & Co., 1910–15), vol. i, p. 146.

Laying Firm Foundations

Roma Agrawal

The many challenges faced by cities like London can, and should, be tackled by engineers. They have the skills at their disposal to design better buildings and infrastructure that meet the needs of its population, especially in the face of growing inequality and the threat of the climate emergency. It might therefore sound strange coming from an engineer – particularly one who is passionate about promoting engineering as a rewarding career choice to young people – that I believe we need to put an end to engineering degrees, at least in the way they currently exist, if we want to build an inclusive London that works for everyone.

During my fourteen-year career as a structural engineer, I was lucky to work on an inspiring range of projects in London, which covered a vast spectrum of scale: from the Shard at London Bridge, ninety-five storeys high, to temporary sculptures in Covent Garden. One thing that always struck me was that most meetings I attended included many other people, regardless of whether our creation was a temporary sculpture in a square, or a skyscraper. I sat among planners, project managers, architects, mechanical, electrical and public health engineers, acoustic specialists, landscape and cost consultants, artists and more. As a collective, we laid out our relevant knowledge, often holding on tightly to our specialism,

From brick terraces and churches to a pinnacle of steel and glass and the extension to a repurposed power station, London's architecture has always been replete with opportunities for the builder and engineer.

ensuring that the scheme we were developing worked well – if not best – from our perspective. In this land of narrow specialisms, inevitably, these perspectives clashed, and then we, as design professionals, had to make compromises – it's a wry observation often made that architects and structural engineers don't get along.

As an engineer, I know there are good reasons why so many specialisms evolved, but what happens in a hundred years' time? With the immense challenges and possibilities that humanity faces, what are the skills and knowledge that are essential for engineers, architects, scientists and all these other professionals? With sophisticated computing likely to be doing the technical heavy lifting, what should the engineer of the future be? My vision is to demolish these silos and the plethora of individual qualifications – yes, even engineering degrees – and focus on the skills and qualities, beyond the technical, of the people who will create the technology and landscape needed for our future.

What might this look like? If we go back in time about 2,000 years, there was no distinction between the architect and the engineer (or any of the other specialists): there was only the master builder. Vitruvius, born about 80–70 BCE, was a Roman master builder who wrote a treatise entitled *De Architectura* (On Architecture). Across its ten volumes Vitruvius records knowledge on town-planning, materials, temples, civil and domestic buildings, and extends the subjects of his writing to include pavements, water supply, astronomy, water mills and hoisting machinery. The first book includes views on the qualifications and skills the architect should have. To modern designers of structures, the inclusion of meteorology, medicine and mathematics may seem strange, but the ancient civilizations – from Harappa (in Punjab), Egypt and China to Europe – were seats of the polymath, the multiskilled designer with a vast breadth of knowledge about construction.

The master builder could not exist in that way today. Vitruvius never had to contend single-handedly with composite materials, 3D-modelling software, complex code, massive or minuscule machinery, and layers of regulation. Technology increases in complexity at an ever faster rate. It's not surprising that now we need a full range of specialisms to design, plan and build our largest infrastructure projects, such as the Elizabeth line or the High Speed 2 (HS2) railway: designers and engineers who understand the nuances of the calculations and judgements they have to make. This, in itself, isn't a problem, but I remain concerned that with narrow specializations in a world that isn't so neatly categorized, we don't have a meaningful understanding of one another's challenges and restraints. Different professionals are brought to a project at different phases, sometimes past the point where their input can truly shape its trajectory. The best design, after all, emerges when we come together at the start of a concept, and work together with empathy.

But there is a problem. We live in a time when circumstances have intensified the need and demand for engineers, but we face a diversity challenge and a skills shortage – there is a lack of people becoming engineers in the first place, particularly those from marginalized backgrounds. I am in a minority of engineers who are women – estimated at 16.5 per cent in the United Kingdom in 2021 – and as a woman of colour I am even more of a rare species – and yes, this has had an impact on my educational and career trajectories.[1] For decades organizations such as the Royal Academy of Engineering have been publishing research that has alerted us to the fact that people from minoritized backgrounds are less likely to study physics, apply for engineering courses, and, even after obtaining degrees, to land job offers and begin careers in engineering. Disproportionate numbers of women drop out of their corporate engineering careers in their thirties and forties – I should know; again, I'm one of them.

The reasons that lead to a lack of engineers in general, and in particular to a lack of diversity, are deep-rooted and complex. If there was a straightforward solution, we would have solved it by now. It starts with the pink for girls and blue for boys divide at birth. I browse the boys' section of shops to buy my daughter clothes with diggers or spaceships on them. Children are forced within the current UK education system to choose between the so-called arts and STEM (science, technology, engineering and mathematics) subjects in their mid-teens, when they are far too young to make a truly informed choice, and find themselves ruled out of some career options. Stereotypes of what engineering has historically been dissuades many from considering it a fulfilling choice. Cultural issues in the workplace lead to problems with the retention of marginalized employees.

Efforts to address this complex landscape of skill and inclusion issues have ranged from grassroots organizations, work in schools, highlighting role models, and corporate social responsibility, to government policy. We are making progress, but it is too slow. We're still missing the seismic shift needed to close the gap so that our engineers reflect our country's diverse

East Bank, a new cultural quarter and 'creative cluster' for the Queen Elizabeth Olympic Park in east London, opens in 2023.

population – and Britain leaving the European Union only compounds this problem. Half the country's population are women, and today about a third of children are from Black, Asian, other minority ethnic or mixed-race backgrounds. The skills shortage that we are facing will become critical if we can't attract and retain women and people of colour.

While we struggle with these issues, the demand for engineers intensifies. To address the climate crisis, we are aiming to achieve a 78 per cent reduction in carbon emissions by 2035, and net zero by 2050. There is intense urbanization as millions of people move into cities. Our lives are becoming increasingly digitized and data-driven. London is already one of the most ethnically diverse cities in the world, so we need to ask ourselves if a workforce that doesn't reflect our population is best placed to take us forwards. We need to question whether designing in the same way that we have done for the last hundred years will lead us to the London that works for us in a hundred years. What materials are right for our future? Should we be prioritizing refurbishment over new build? How do we cope with the increasing demands on our housing and infrastructure? We've just emerged from a global pandemic, which has had far-reaching effects

Children learning about structures at the Royal Academy Lego Challenge, part of the London Festival of Architecture in June 2019.

on our healthcare, ways of working and the shape of our homes. There are leaps in technology, with machine learning and artificial intelligence. We are producing and collecting data as never before, and technology such as quantum computing promises to disrupt our digital landscape beyond recognition. But the construction sector seems to lag behind on adopting cutting-edge innovation on a large scale.

Given that we need more engineers to work on climate change, infrastructure, healthcare, food production and a host of other challenges, and given that we are currently struggling to hire and retain enough engineers, it might sound pretty controversial that I'm suggesting doing away with engineering degrees and qualifications. The reason I say this is because even if a student has navigated the many forks in their educational path that lead to engineering, it is still a very confusing field. The way in which engineering is split into separate disciplines – structural, mechanical, chemical and so many, many more – is not sustainable. Already we are seeing the lines between these specialisms being blurred: where does a renewable energy expert who focuses on biochemical power sit, for example? It's also inevitable that advances in computing techniques will mean that our jobs will be less about detailed, individual, technical design – the months I spent designing beams individually on the Shard more than a decade ago will be reduced to seconds – and more about working creatively as a team to generate ideas and test them in order to solve problems well. I believe that rather than obtaining qualifications in a narrow section of engineering, our future workforce should be trained in a full breadth of topics that will put humans and our planet at the centre of the design of our cities. To answer the hard questions, we need to understand how power plays out in society, so isn't it imperative that we study ethics, law, social mobility, sustainability and more? By erasing the lines between all the current specialisms, we can attract more people into our industry, people who may not see themselves as engineers, but as multiskilled designers of the built environment.

In this way we can move towards a new version of the Vitruvian engineer, a version inspired by children, who play and tinker with, throw, break and touch everything they can see to understand their surroundings better, without boundaries, without fear, driven purely by curiosity. Rather than focusing on the differences in the minutiae of knowledge needed by an architect, structural engineer or quantity surveyor, let's consider the characteristics a person needs in order to build our city better, and let's centre the education system on these. We must prioritize people and the planet. We must interrogate our history: how London was formed and why, and the impact of this on how its citizens live today. We must theorize about the future: what are the small and big questions we will need to consider? And we must study the present: what are the forces that shape society today? Let's take engineering towards a more philosophical and social approach, and create the best London for 2123.

Note

1 'New Analysis Shows Increase of Women Working in Engineering', EngineeringUK, 3 March 2022, www.engineeringuk.com/news-views/new-analysis-shows-increase-of-women-working-in-engineering.

A City of High Streets

Mark Brearley

A while ago I spent some time in a big Dutch new town. It's one that's doing reasonably well, and all is very green and neat. But the place is odd, in a way that we've all experienced before. Something seems to be missing, because it's been hidden away. The shy creature, skulking out of view beyond the trees, is the economy. The office blocks and the industry are off on their own, landscaped and screened. The schools, colleges and healthcare buildings lurk around the back on quiet suburban roads. Shops and community centres, and the places to get a meal or a drink, are in little precincts that you go to when you need to, and only then. It feels as though the town turned out that way because people had in mind an idea that the economy is a thing that others do for you, or do to you, that it is okay for it to be over there, not here, and that there is no need for it to be exposed.

That Dutch planned place would have been emerging from the soil during the years when I first spent time in London, in the 1970s, as a teenager. Not long after that I made the move south to the capital, hunting for success. I came from the suburban south of Manchester, an area then adjusting fast to the pace and scale of the car, and to me London felt surprisingly old-fashioned. I found a city like the one captivatingly described by my grandparents, who had spent their younger years in the then flourishing and intense Gorton and Denton areas of Manchester. This city showed itself to the world, with its economy and public goings-on evident to all; it was the joyful opposite of the car-based and fractured urbanism of the Manchester suburbs, and of the Dutch considered and predrawn version. What I was seeing was a city of high streets, with an extrovert economy.

London is a huge conurbation throughout which much of what goes on, and much of what its inhabitants all share, is clustered around the streets where people and vehicles flow. I am now convinced that this time-battered urban structure, which for so long seemed anachronistic, is our city's most prized urban asset for the future, and a key to the ongoing success of its economy, its civic life and its social dynamic. It is also a rich reference point for the tomorrows of many cities around the world as they grow and regenerate themselves.

Taken together, London's 600 high streets (yes, that's six hundred) are a vast phenomenon, and so everyday that we forget to notice them as remarkable. Place them all end-to-end and they would extend for about 500 kilometres (310 miles), from Highbury Corner up the Great North Road and all the way to the Scottish border. It would take three weeks to walk its length, if you kept your pace up, and each step of the way you would pass a vibrant and prominent economy, sometimes rough, struggling, battered, but as often prosperous, sparkling, improving. Some parts are thin, just a shallow crust around the residential areas beyond, but elsewhere the people-filled ways fold and loop, along side roads, rear streets, arcades and malls, big lobbies and foyers, yards, estates and multiuser buildings, with workspace and industry, offices and trade counters.

These high-street places contain much more than just shops; indeed, not far off half the jobs are from a catalogue of other activities. This is where London is at its most effervescent and available, and that includes what's around the back too, hidden away and humdrum, such as along Hassop Road in Cricklewood, with its dozens of car fixers, running parallel to Cricklewood Broadway. If you take a walk east along the route that runs for 51 kilometres (32 miles) across London from Uxbridge to Romford, via Oxford Street, for example, you will find the front doors of about 5,500 businesses and institutions, where some 80,000 people work. That's as many as work at Canary Wharf, just on one sample strip. Between them, London's high-street places (outside the city's centre) are home to nearly 1.5 million jobs: 35 per cent of all the jobs in London. In these high streets there are almost twice as many businesses and other organizations employing people as can be found in the centre, and nearly 60 per cent of the whole city's small and medium-sized enterprises. These settings are entrepreneurial, economically diverse and staggeringly extensive.

Tottenham also has a car-repair cluster, its equivalent of Cricklewood's unsung wonder, tucked behind the High Road north of White Hart Lane station. Go there and you'll see a nicely mixed part of London, rich in many ways, even though battered and short on prosperity, and certainly you can procure what's needed for most of life within only a short walk. Gathered around the old run of high streets heading towards Hertford, alongside the shops and cafés, there is a library, the town hall, a swimming pool and gyms, the police station, advice places and easy-access office spaces. Away from the street frontage, close by the car fixers, is a high-quality wholesale bakery, along with some new small breweries, a wood miller, a big new supermarket and a college. Over to the east, a short walk into the industrial areas, there's the factory that makes military dress uniforms and another that produces bespoke light fittings, as well as the Gina luxury shoe factory, the big pitta bakeries, the artists' studios, the printers, patisseries, joiners and metal fabricators, cash-and-carries and trade warehouses. There are plenty of places to worship, to hear and make music, to play pool. There are pubs and clubs, schools and colleges, banks, a post office, a couple of markets, many haircuts to be had, and a newly built football stadium, its vastness entered via the high street. This is a locality with plenty of problems, where riots flared up as recently as 2011, where there is deprivation and dysfunction. But it is also a superb host for enterprise, organized in a way that you could plan only in your dreams.

It is the visible high-street-hooked economy in such places that incidentally teaches and inspires as it goes about its daily exchanges. Our high streets welcome so many of the productive things we do together, to provide one another with the essentials and the luxuries; they host a bewildering array of interdependent activities, evident to all, that encourage us to act with enthusiasm and initiative, each in our own way, as part of that vast self-driven effort, the city and its economy. London's hundreds of high streets are our city's most remarkable typicality, one that should be not only better recognized and cherished, but also actively nurtured and evolved. London has Britain's oldest high street, it is the city that invented the modern high street, and in spite of concerted efforts

Cranbourn Street, Covent Garden.

to undermine them, and even though we have neglected to notice, it's still structured around these great arteries, where so much of life comes together.[1] This battered matrix is a colossal lucky find. So much more is possible if we work to enrich and enlarge it, if we can grasp the potential, shift attitudes, usher in a fresh ambition for our city's future. It's a good-city idea that's been hiding in plain sight: *the city of high streets*.

The timing for refreshing our London-of-tomorrow objectives is perfect. We have been witnessing the surprise crumbling of a consensus that mobility by roads is pivotal. A global shift, the receding of that agreement, is underway; it's unmistakable, even though still fragile, but what's creating a tipping point is its correlation with the increasing popularity of urban lifestyles. While reasoned critique of twentieth-century assumptions about mobility has been persistent since the late 1950s (the urbanist and writer Jane Jacobs started working on her book *The Death and Life of Great American Cities* in 1958, and it came out in 1961), it has taken until today, more than sixty years later, for aspiration to factor in on a sufficient scale to change the main trajectory, in places such as London, and for it to start to feel as though the long process of urban disaggregation has slowed, and could even be reversing. If we stand back and notice that this spontaneous moderation of the role of the car is happening, it's possible to recognize that the city of this century could look very different from the way we long imagined it would. London has welcomed this change, has worked hard to accelerate it and has put great efforts into a long-term recalibration of street space. But a broader adjustment of city-shaping aims is so far conspicuously missing.

Useful ideas have been bubbling up, though. Strongly heard of late, and music to my ears, are calls for the 15-minute city: with all the facilities we need to live successful and sustainable lifestyles within a short walk of everyone's home. It's a compelling look ahead to that less car-focused future, implying the requirement for a fine-grained blend of uses across the city. But that aim needs a configuration; it begs questions about how best to arrange so much localized provision, to consider how we should organize the array of accommodation required to host diverse goings-on, and to decide whether to scatter or bunch, hide or present.

Well, luckily for us in London, as if by magic, the city arrangements that seem most appropriate for this century's very different version of tomorrow are already there, battered and belittled, but still ready for us to mould. The objective should be to magnify the gathering of life around mixed streets that are part of a wider urban continuity, and in the depth behind and beyond. *The city of high streets* is the configuration idea that can guide us as we evolve a city in which moving and arriving blur, marrying the local and the metropolitan in a way that shares, gifting endless opportunities to those who can fully enjoy the ease of travel our city offers, while also providing for those who don't or can't. These are places of exchange, threaded through London, with an open civic and economic life.

But today we hear tales of high-street shrinkage: the argument that because online selling is reducing the shop space needed per person, it's desirable to sweep away capacity, to retrench. The planners, ever hunting for their housing numbers, claim additional justification for long-cherished trim-and-compact policies, ushering in the housebuilders, looking the other way as our most remarkable urban typicality becomes embattled and eroded, its depth-accommodation removed and its tentacles snipped. Look with more care, though, and the trends point elsewhere, to the need for affirmation and expansion. The recalibration of retail is counterbalanced across most of London by growing demand that comes with more population. We have been seeing a fast increase in the number of people going out to be served food and drink, and a blossoming preference for working in shared Wi-Fi-enabled spaces, together with a new mood of public conviviality. Meanwhile, surprise trends include the resurgence of cinemas, a gym boom and bakeries roaring back. Alongside new awareness of a need for more local repairers, just-in-time preparers, producers, suppliers and carriers, we are seeing strong demand for smaller-scale industrial premises to host all these.

The nut to crack is sturdier, though; it's not just a matter of pointing out trend misreadings and that a singular focus on the virtues of housing development is not desirable. Some more deeply embedded mindsets must be shifted. This became evident to me during my years working for the Mayor of London. It was 2010, and the person leading preparation of the *London Plan* started to express alarm that my team's investigations into London's high streets, and their potential for the future, were starting to hit at the heart of that city plan, and of town-planning ideas in general. He had a go at warning us to stop pushing the way we were, and his salvo contained references to the nineteenth-century economist Johann Heinrich von Thünen, the twentieth-century geographer Walter Christaller, the twentieth-century town planner Sir Patrick Abercrombie, and the broader

The Broadway, Southall.

history of planning, while I thought 'Gotcha!'[2] At that moment, fear of long-cherished notions being overturned came to the surface, and it became clear that ingrained attitudes were sustaining the disregard of London's most breathtakingly potential-rich urban phenomenon.

It was the urbanist Clarence Perry who came up with the 'neighbourhood unit' concept for the planning of functional, self-contained and desirable neighbourhoods in industrializing cities, such as his own Chicago in the 1920s.[3] The sub-urbanized approach he advocated is typical of the city-shaping ideas that were dominant throughout the twentieth century, ideas that surface energetically in such documents as the 1940s *County of London Plan* and the 1960s *Greater London Development Plan*, and are still there shouting at us from the current *London Plan*, as though time has stood still. Some see the Abercrombie-steered *County of London Plan* as an inspirational and benign outcome of the first blossoming of town-planning in the United Kingdom.[4] But, whenever you might be tempted by its charming self-assurance, it's good to look through the 1945 *Penguin County of London Plan Explained by E.J. Carter and Ernő Goldfinger* for a reminder that the vision expressed therein is a variant of Perry's clunky notion, and that it required the mass destruction of London's high streets. The authors of the *County of London Plan* sought the city as tree, one of separate single-community leaves; they proposed a conurbation without high streets and their capacity to host.[5] Their version of good, their enthusiasm for segregating our city into free-floating chunks, forcing ruptures, putting travelling and being-there on to different pages, has refused to go away; it still lurks, not only in the *London Plan*, but also in each borough plan, even though at last we can see forwards to the alternatives. Now seems like the time to call out those ideas as unwanted, to put them to bed, then look again at the city we have and affirm anew its immanent structure.

I'm urging a bold strategy that rejects consolidation and the willingness to trim, and seeks to halt the denuding of our city's high-street matrix, seeing off the decades-long efforts to turn a rich weave into a pattern of spots, abandoning the notion of 'town centres' and the belief in high-street decline that needs managing. Instead we should embrace high streets as a big organizational idea; we should assume substantial high-street growth as London flourishes, with those settings encouraged and enabled to expand, to become more fully welcoming. We can incrementally reshape a London structured around its mixed and vibrant filigree.

As well as the shopping, the eating and the drinking, high streets should be where the public rooms we use for events and meetings are grouped; where clubs, classes, faith and community concentrate; where we go to send and collect packages, take care of our looks and our bodies, and find places for youth, for all that working on laptops and smartphones, for possibilities to sit and watch the world go by. The scarcity of land in London has forced the designers of new schools and other civic buildings to innovate, taking us back to the more compact urban formats that fell from popularity long ago. Those ways of building are more suited to high streets, joyfully facing outwards, rather than lying low on rear roads; so let's say that in future most of our collective buildings, including our schools, colleges and meeting places, should be entered from the high street. When we see a refreshing of local democracy and decision-making dialogue, for that, too, high streets are the natural context, and they should offer space for smaller workshops and workrooms for mending and servicing, assembling in wood and metal, printing, preparing food, for start-up producers and hobby-makers. It is in each locality's high street that we need the builders' merchants, equipment hirers and the delicate tassels of logistics networks.

To set us off on the journey, we must open up a broader discussion about what sort of city we want. That could be enabled by the Greater

London Authority and local authorities, as they have a go at getting their planners out of ruts trundled in for too long. If that took us to an embrace of *the city of high streets* as a guiding ambition, there would need to be a careful process of changing policy and adjusting aims. A first step could be to give protective planning designation to the 70 per cent of London's high streets that are currently outside it, and hence vulnerable to strip-out, and to make clear that the new objective is to extend, cultivate, nurture and connect, to halt the erosion of London's high streets, to shift towards increasing the range of accommodation, giving an energetic push to innovative development types and combinations of uses, spreading a refreshed understanding of the dynamics of public choice, footfall, frontage and depth. We can go after a city with an unbroken high-street lattice, with places of exchange that wend their way through each of those 600 localities.

As our high streets evolve, they can grow and become even more of a focus for the burgeoning city: more intense, fun and cared about, more alive and extraordinary. Our notion of what makes a good city is shifting. The last century does today feel like a distant past. At last it seems possible to say farewell to the whole bundle of twentieth-century city-shaping ideas. So long Perry, Abercrombie, Buchanan,[6] Van Eesteren and the *Athens Charter*,[7] circles and segregation, garden cities, (drive-in) garden centres, (drive-to) shopping centres, town centres, leisure centres, community and neighbourhood centres. Hello high-street places, longer and deeper, use-full, linchpin of the new metropolitan spirit and an organic refreshing of the civic, a way forwards for the city of continuities and mix, an extrovert and shared city. We thought we would have to hunt far and wide, but oh happy realization, there it is on Tottenham High Road, that big urban idea for the current century, *the city of high streets*.

Notes

1 Whitechapel High Street has a plausible claim to a 2,000-year history. It must be admitted, though, that Colchester High Street, at the other end of the Romans' Great Road from Aldgate to Colchester, may be similarly ancient.

2 Thünen's model of agricultural land use, published in 1826 as *Der isolierte Staat* (The Isolated State), set out methods of maximizing agricultural production in concentric zones. Christaller's principal contribution to the discipline is central place theory, first proposed in his *Central Places in Southern Germany* (1933).

3 Clarence A. Perry, *The Neighborhood Unit: A Scheme of Arrangement for the Family-life Community*, Monograph One in *Neighborhood and Community Planning, Regional Plan of New York and Its Environs* (Committee on Regional Plan of New York and Its Environs, 1929).

4 John Henry Forshaw and Sir Leslie Patrick Abercrombie, *County of London Plan* (Macmillan, 1943).

5 My mention of 'city as tree' references Christopher Alexander's *A City Is Not a Tree* [1965] (Thames & Hudson, 1988; repr. Sustasis Press, 2015), which I heartily recommend.

6 The town and traffic planner Sir Colin Buchanan wrote *Traffic in Towns* (HMSO, 1963), in which he set out policy blueprints for adjusting urban environments in response to the mass use of motor cars; the suggestions, which assumed substantial urban redevelopment, included traffic containment and segregation, new corridor and distribution roads, precincts and environmental areas.

7 The architect and town planner Cornelis van Eesteren strongly advocated the idea of the 'functional city', in which the various functions – among them living, working, traffic, nature and recreation – are separated. The architect Le Corbusier popularized the concept further through his *Athens Charter* document of 1933.

Idlewild Mews (2022), by vPPR architects, is a development of eight affordable homes for Croydon Council making use of an old garage site that would have been of no interest to a traditional developer.

Wrap It Up and Start Again
The Future of London's Housing

Claire Bennie

In the original *London of the Future* publication from 1921, W.R. Davidge (a former housing commissioner) foresaw many of the changes that were to take place in his view of housing within the boundaries of London. He identified and bemoaned the onset of the capital's 'ugly' suburban sprawl: 'in all the suburbs there has been a steady creeping paralysis of two-story [*sic*] villadom, mile after mile of brick and mortar slowly eating up the country-side.'[1] There was regret expressed at the continuing unhealthy overcrowding in the centre of 1920s London. Some of the author's proposed solutions came to pass, starting about twenty-five years later. With political will perhaps galvanized by the aftermath of war, a 'green belt' was introduced to combat sprawl. London attempted to solve 'overspill' outside its curtilage in a few notable New Towns, which attracted pioneer Londoners willing to leave the city for the promise of a new and better life.

Yet sprawl burgeoned beyond the author's wildest nightmares and, despite the substantial amount of social housing built in the middle of the twentieth century, overcrowding and poor condition of stock are still with us. Post-war population shrinkage radically reversed in London in the early 1990s, largely driven by the increase in the number of financial-sector jobs. And while the hundred-year doubling of the capital's housing stock absorbed some of that growth, the same period saw a near-halving of the number of people living in each of those homes. London's 3.6 million homes still appear to be under pressure; but what now for housing supply and demand in the capital in the wake of Brexit and the COVID-19 pandemic?

The year 2023 feels like a very unstable vantage point from which to answer that question. On the face of it, home building is still not keeping up with demand. We appear to be back in an era in which, despite the qualitative ambitions of the *London Plan* of 2021, numbers are 'our blinding passion', as the pioneering social housing expert Elizabeth Denby put it.[2] Land in the capital is expensive. Build costs are spiralling. Developers are pushing building heights on every plot. They're building flats almost exclusively – both in the centre of London and in the suburbs – and debates are raging about whether the increasing number of tall blocks are good for either residents or places. We may not all find this comfortable, but these surely aren't signs of a London in retreat? Or does the pausing of major new infrastructure such as Crossrail 2 and the Bakerloo line extension signal a different future?

This essay, a brief survey of London's housing future, will begin with a look at possible trajectories of its population and household composition, and lead to ideas about where and how new homes might be built. It will conclude by addressing the two biggest problems of London housing – affordability and sustainability. Climate change is perhaps the only certainty we can and must plan for.

The Greater London Authority (GLA) projects that despite the pandemic-induced population downturn, London's population is already growing again and may add two million people by the middle of the twenty-first century (a slower rate of growth than since 1990). This continued rise may seem counter-intuitive, given the current transition to remote working and the cost of living in London, as well as uncertainty about international migration and the future of London's economy post-Brexit. The pandemic has accelerated the dislocation of jobs and homes forever for about a third of the working population. That's 1.5 million Londoners who in theory could be somewhere else, though many may still be drawn to the London magnet by family, friends and myriad cultural offerings. International migration as a feature of London's short-term future growth is very unclear; most commentary suggests that calculating 'births minus deaths' is the more likely net population contributor. But will there be anything for all these new Londoners to do? Diverse forecasts for London's economy and jobs are impossible to interpret so soon after a major economic shock. The GLA is predicting medium-term economic growth for the capital, in spite of Brexit and a national refocus on the regions. And perhaps they're right – London got through a plague, fire and blitz, as the cliché goes. Longer term, London may experience more international migration as climate change renders more of the world uninhabitable – a topic explored further below. So we can probably assume that London's population has not peaked yet.

The implication of two million more Londoners is, of course, more homes. Is there room for a million more homes in London, to add to the existing 3.6 million? The GLA thinks so, and has published that in its *London Plan*. But the game of 'fitting more homes into London' is getting harder to play. The city's growth has historically occurred through boundary expansion into green fields as well as through slum clearance, remediating bombsites and repurposing defunct industrial land. The capital's boundary is now proving stubborn, with the Green Belt (much of it inaccessible) seen as untouchable. 'Intensification' is now the watchword, but that's a highly contested activity. The next fifty years are likely to see homes built on roofs, on car parks and on former industrial land. Housing estates may continue to be redeveloped, but this way of adding new homes can be unacceptably costly both in terms of embodied carbon and community fracture. Some predict suburban intensification through resident-led redevelopment, but will individual households really coalesce as first-time developers and strike land deals with small-scale developers? Perhaps the 25 per cent of London's land that is currently back garden could be pressed into service. Or is it finally time to set out some brave new policy by asking our best designers to create high-quality, carbon-positive homes in the Green Belt?

Numbers are only part of the future housing scene: the types and arrangements of homes in which Londoners live also have a material impact on their quality of life. In some ways, homes themselves have changed surprisingly little over the centuries. What are homes, in essence? They are places for a discrete family unit to cook, eat, sleep, wash, play, relax and store their ever-burgeoning 'stuff' behind a lockable door. Now, through the tragedy of digital technology, they are also places to work, shop and access almost any information or entertainment the inhabitants could possibly want. No one needs to leave their home ever again in order to live. Moving beyond the individual unit, the way in which those homes

The focus of La Borda cooperative housing development (2018) in Barcelona, by Lacol, is on the value of its use, rather than speculation on its value in the market.

are laid out and managed can make a surprising amount of difference to human flourishing. London has an equal mix of flats and houses, built at various heights and in various formats, suggesting that there is something for all tastes. But are London's existing and emerging homes actually fit for our current or future demographics, and what should be done if not?

Space standards in London – whether for existing or new homes – are notoriously meagre compared to those of most other Western cities, and with the advent of homeworking, these standards are now problematic for many. Office floorspace has been notionally redistributed to our homes, but there's been no associated redistribution of wealth to allow the rental or purchase of a new home with that crucial extra 10 square metres (108 square feet). The home ownership cohort in London will undoubtedly extend upwards and into their gardens, or just purchase more space. But what will the renters (half of London's households) do? It would be interesting to see estates, old and new, where rentable workspace became an integral part of the accommodation mix, with rents paid by employers. Such local workspace may actually be better off on the capital's many high streets, making the dormitory suburbs into thriving villages again. The obvious danger is a hollowing out of London's many centres – but perhaps homes will begin to appear in converted office space there once the workplace spasm has abated.

Shared living models are gaining some attention in other parts of the world, but are they a part of London's future? The nearly million Londoners who live alone may find the long-term cost of solitude prohibitive in terms of both practicalities (rent and bills) and their well-being. Young Londoners are beginning to benefit from purpose-built rental blocks – now comprising every sixth new home – with amenities to suit their lifestyles. But older Londoners are the least well served by London's housing stock, which is largely inaccessible, hard to heat and the wrong size for their life-stage. Co-housing models for older people are currently a fringe typology which needs to be enabled and mainstreamed in the capital. Applying these models would free up family houses for the many who need them, releasing 2.75 million spare rooms (and a value of £200 billion) back into full-time use.

A final observation about housing types in London must concern the high-rise block, scourge of many a suburban planning committee. High-rise flats may appear a panacea, maximizing housing numbers, enabling social and commercial infrastructure, and providing views and light to residents. Opposing views usually run as follows. High-rise living is suitable only for perhaps 5 per cent of the population: primarily those without children and the wealthy. High rise is expensive to build, expensive to maintain and energy-hungry, making it a profligate building type, in spite of its land efficiency. And finally, some Londoners resent the visual and environmental impact of high rise on their largely low-rise city. In East Asia, and latterly in Toronto and Melbourne, high rise has been embraced as a mainstay of city-centre living. Will London continue to go the same way? It may well do so in the short term, but only because the inevitable urban trade-off between quantity of life and quality of life will have fallen towards the former. There is currently no rigour in comparative long-term cost and sustainability data for high-rise versus lower-rise flats. A future London where high rise has been abandoned due to prohibitive upkeep and running costs is not fanciful.

The causes of housing non-affordability in London are disputed, some citing undersupply of homes in general, with others pointing to rock-bottom mortgage interest rates raising values beyond the means of many. If we believe the 'scarcity' camp, three reasons given for London's undersupply are an absolute lack of land, restrictive planning policy, and excessive numbers of empty or visitor lets. Clearly there is less available land in London than there was in the previous hundred years, but might we soon see obsolescence of space in the commercial sector? The idea that planning policy greatly constrains supply is vehemently contested – would the market really deliver substantially more if allowed to let rip? The Green Belt is the most obvious constraint, and only 4 per cent of it could yield a million homes, according to some. Short-term rentals of entire homes, via such online platforms as Airbnb, and the practice of 'buy to leave', or purchasing properties as investments and leaving them unoccupied, are tying up more than 130,000 London properties (1.25 per cent and 2.5 per cent respectively of the total London stock). Changing policy in these areas would be a move towards a more equitable city, but would not cause a major adjustment to affordability in the capital.

The demand-side camp firmly asserts that the non-affordability of housing in London is mainly caused by numerous factors: global city status, wealth distribution, cheap mortgages, tax incentives, tech-enabled visitor demand and some job-related population growth. Radical external shocks or new policies would be required to rock London demand: are these coming? London's market renters – 26 per cent of residents – are the ones least well served. Their wages have stagnated, their housing benefit has been cut and social housing is disappearing. Their security of tenure and minimum home quality standard are both shockingly poor. All these issues could and should be fixed now, never mind in the next hundred years. Things may get sticky soon for the homeowners too. External global factors pushing interest rates up and overseas investment down could cause structural change to values in the next ten years. Remote working may yet redistribute dwellers from London's grip to places further afield. Longer term, it's far from clear how the concentration of wealth among older generations will trickle through to the young. Who will be able to buy all these half-a-million-pound homes in twenty years' time?

Both camps agree that increasing the supply of institutional low-rent homes would be a good idea. In 1921 municipal housing was in its infancy (spurred and funded by the Addison Act of 1919, which promised government subsidy for 500,000 council houses within three years), with only 1 per cent of the London population being housed by the London County Council and local authorities. Public-sector housing peaked in 1981 at 35 per cent of homes in London, before falling to 21 per cent in 2022 (mostly as a result of 'right to buy'). The cry often understandably goes up: 'we should just build more council housing.' It's hard to argue with this, but the gap in funding needed to build the desired 30,000 affordable homes per year in London is £7.5 billion, which is not currently on offer. £200 billion then, to double London's existing affordable housing stock, and no ability for London to raise that subsidy from its wealth-making business and financial sector. Others in this book will speculate as to whether London's devolution is a sensible solution to its problems.

The whole of the above narrative may be rendered entirely irrelevant by the impacts wrought by climate change, which is without doubt the single most significant life-changing issue of the coming century. Its relatively slow onset (compared, say, to that of the pandemic) is unfortunate: politicians appear unable to enact the radical policies required to reverse the effects because there is no immediate catastrophic outcome. The building industry is barely waking up to its own contribution: conferences abound, policies exist, but design and building practice remains stubbornly wasteful and detrimental. London's existing housing stock is poorly insulated and the longer-term impacts of climate change could be wide-ranging, from overheating through to flooding and inward migration.

The only correct way to start mitigation is to reduce the demand for energy and the use of virgin materials. Retrofitting the whole of London's stock to a meaningful standard would cost in the order of £100,000 per older home, giving a total cost of £200 billion, or £22,000 per head. (This compares with pandemic spending at about £5,000 per head.) More draconian, and likely to be politically unpalatable, would be to constrain household energy use, although the prohibitive cost of energy may be the most powerful incentive most people need. We may end up living in a single insulated room in our homes in the winter. The 2.6 million cars parked outside London's homes are already reducing in number, but many of those homes require far better access to public transport. Car-dependent homes may lose their value, as might the 10 per cent of homes in London's flood-risk areas, though the Thames Barrier looks set to do its job for some time yet. Migration to London from the rest of the world is a longer-term possibility, as the proportion of global land area rendered uninhabitable is set to increase from 1 per cent to 19 per cent by 2070 and

The Hoxton Press Buildings (2018), a primarily residential development in Hoxton, east London, by David Chipperfield Architects and Karakusevic Carson Architects.

migrants tend to go to cities. However, climate migrants are more likely to move within their continent long before taking the drastic step to go overseas.

So after all that, which scenarios emerge? Climate change could propel London in two radically different directions. Extraordinary levels of global migration could cause us to provide a whole new generation of homes in London and its wider hinterland. Conversely, a draconian clamp-down on resource use would stop us building anything new at all. The first scenario is akin to a bursting dam: temporary homes proliferate, planning laws become more permissive (or are routinely broken) and infrastructure (and social relations) are under severe pressure. Big incentives are provided for underoccupiers to take in refugees. Systems for erecting small prefab houses develop to help local authorities and others deliver at speed – think of the assembly line of the temporary Nightingale Hospitals constructed during the pandemic. But would all this be happening in London itself? It feels more likely that London's Green Belt and the outskirts of southeastern towns would take the strain, much as they did when post-war 'London overspill' translated into 'expanded towns' such as Swindon in Wiltshire. The second scenario – effectively a de-growth model – is in fact far more radical, and perhaps even more feared. There is a ban on the use of all virgin materials. Demolition is forbidden without explicit justification. A major retrofit programme is instigated. New builds must be carbon-positive. Energy and travel are rationed. Even if ethically 'right', this entirely new paradigm would need a profound public health shock to bring it about.

Perhaps in every era, essayists have suffered from the hubris of imagining themselves and their city to be on the brink of great change or disaster. It therefore feels ill-advised to conjure up, as did the novelist J.G. Ballard, a future for London consisting of riots, refugees, starvation or abandoned real estate. But equally it's hard to imagine that climate change is not going to catalyse a revolution, both social and industrial, over the next century. Rather than another hundred-year doubling of London's housing stock, the focus must surely turn to the more urgent task – making London's existing homes sustainable. Now our first act must be to create an environment where a high calibre of political leaders can emerge to guide us through these very challenging options.

Afterthought

It's interesting to note that £200 billion is the value trapped in London's spare rooms. It's also the cost of doubling the capital's affordable housing stock or of retrofitting its homes. I wonder how many in the older generation might contemplate funding one of those two important initiatives through their wills?

Notes

1 W.R. Davidge, 'The Housing of London' in *London of the Future* (E.P. Dutton & Co., 1921), p. 200.

2 Elizabeth Denby, *Europe Re-housed* (George Allen & Unwin, 1938), p. 11.

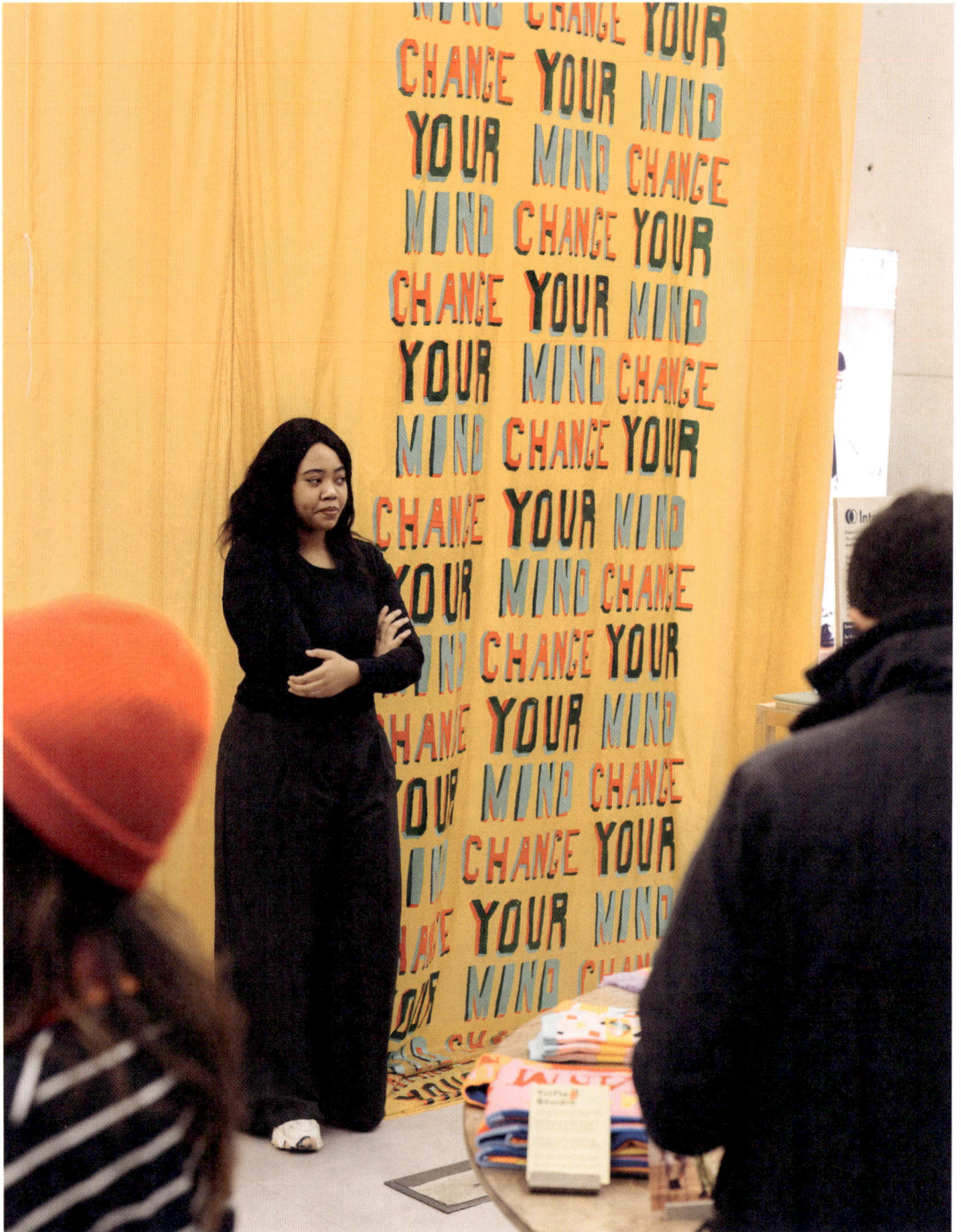

An event held at Lab E20, London's flagship creative community hub for the circular economy and regenerative design, in December 2022. Lab E20 was founded by Yasmin Jones-Henry and the fashion designer Christopher Raeburn for the developer Get Living as part of the regeneration of the Olympic Park. The artwork is *Change Your Mind* by Trifle Studio artist Andre Williams.

Inclusive by Design

Yasmin Jones-Henry

As a cultural practitioner and writer, I'm passionate about curating narratives and spaces that invite further discourse on sustainability and design, while making the economic case for culture. The term 'cultural placemaking' has been thrown about as a piece of jargon by local authorities and property developers. It is misconceived as being an afterthought of urban design to help developers sell more commercial leases, but it means so much more than that. Cultural placemaking will be the conduit for London's metamorphosis into its future self.

What is 'cultural placemaking'?

When done properly, cultural placemaking is as much about introducing new systems and ways of thinking as it is about conserving culture and heritage. It's about identifying, amplifying and underlining the true DNA structures of what makes our cities and communities the best they can possibly be. This is why I believe London's distinctive culture will be not only the catalyst, but also the custodian of the capital's reputation as a world-class destination for investment and regenerative design, and a place of diversity.

The United Nations' Sustainable Development Goals (UN SDGs) for 2030 have realigned the framework upon which future growth in our global, national and local economies will be measured. They further provide the criteria for which the future of urban design, product design and place will be defined. UN SDG 11 seeks to build 'Sustainable Cities and Communities'.[1] Assuming it has surpassed the UN's 2030 target for a low-carbon and circular economy, the London of the future that I would like to imagine, therefore, is one that is described as 'inclusive by design'.

Looking beyond the current political and economic turmoil, the London of the future that I foresee is as follows.

Diversity is our superpower

The diversity I refer to here is not only the well-documented 2,000-year-old legacy of multiculturalism, migration and cultural integration for which this city is already known. Neither do I wish to focus this particular narrative on race. The diversity I speak of is reflected in London's aesthetic and economy. The London of 2023 is woefully underperforming in representing neurodiversity and disability in its growing population. According to the disability equality charity Scope, 'Attitudes towards disabled people are often poorer in London … We have already seen that a person's proximity to a disabled person can have [a positive] impact on their attitudes towards disability.'[2]

The correlation between a lack of inclusion and a rise in prejudice is also manifested through design. Accessibility and inclusivity must be the defining features of the London of the future – from the way in which we design our public realm to the way in which we regulate and invest in urban design. Ella Ritchie, founder of Intoart (which opened Trifle Studio, London's first commercial design studio for differently abled artisans), observes: 'People with learning disabilities are rarely thought of as cultural producers in the design industry, which is a missed opportunity for everyone.'[3] Furthermore, a report in 2019 by the US business news website Quartz notes that: 'According to one study, the total disposable income of the [disabled] community tops $8 trillion [£6.6 trillion in 2023] per year. For context that makes the community third largest in the world in terms of purchasing power after the USA and China.'[4]

My sincere hope is that the London of the future will have woken up to the untapped resource, potential and creativity latent within this underserved demographic. Organizations such as Intoart and its initiative Trifle Studio, working from their London campuses, will have redrawn the landscape in collaboration with developers and local councils, bringing their community of neurodiverse and highly commercially successful artisans into placeshaping's bigger conversations across urban design, architecture and creative enterprise.

Within my own work as a strategist, sitting between creatives and investors, I do my best to bring the relevant stakeholders into the room when the early design conversations at masterplan level take place. My hope is also that the London of the future progresses beyond its existing reputation for finance and technology, and finds a new comparative advantage in social value through co-creation and co-design. The London of the future will be a co-designed capital, bringing with it a collective share in civic pride, a genuine sense of belonging, and a combined sense of responsibility to conserve what we've built together, the environment and our communities.

Diversity of thought: The '5 Cs'

To apply a term pioneered by my former boss and placemaking pioneer Mark Davy, founder of the placemaking agency Futurecity, London will be a paradigm for other global cities in its use of the '5 Cs' approach. This positions culture at the intersection where London's commercial, civic, community and consumer stakeholders are able to collaborate in a truly inclusive and transparent way. I believe the application of this approach will be the antidote to gentrification and the habitual erasure of minority community groups whenever areas of London have previously experienced redevelopment.

Whether it is used to contribute to the design of residential, commercial and cultural spaces, or to that of London's green spaces and public realm, the 5 Cs approach will reveal the dividends of social and commercial value that are generated when previously divided stakeholders come together to agree on concept, ideation, delivery and access.

With productivity driven by a fully circular economy, an organic clustering of London's core industries, services and businesses will create natural economies of scale, enabling the further development of a low-carbon, low-emissions, 15-minute city. Quality of life, commuting and affordability within the city will have been resolved as each cluster will have evolved with mixed-use developments combining commercial, community and residential spaces. Creative-tech, visual art and film will all grow in their capacity to absorb and amplify new and exciting stories. London's collective of creatives will use the art of storytelling to rehabilitate and empower their local communities.

Organizations such as the Raindance Film School, the British Film Institute and the British Academy of Film and Television Arts (BAFTA) will have expanded their footprint beyond Soho, the South Bank and Piccadilly to work across the boroughs, local schools and community centres. This will enable the expansion of London's grassroots, independent film industry, bringing international visitors to witness the city's world-class talent. London's film and technology sectors will also drive further innovation into multisensory cultural consumption, widening accessibility in storytelling and shared experiences in public and private spaces. The British Fashion Council's Institute of Positive Fashion will have grown its global audience for London designers generating innovative material solutions – provoking further cross-sector collaborations between fintech, biotech and creative-tech.

The London of the future will still – after 2,000 years – be an inherently tribal city. The age-old north-versus-south, east-versus-west rivalries will continue to thrive. Only now, in 2123, the competition is across creative clusters: that established in west London by the West London Alliance (consisting of the borough councils of Barnet, Brent, Ealing, Hammersmith & Fulham, Harrow, Hillingdon and Hounslow); East Bank and the Fashion District (covering the east London boroughs of Newham, Hackney, Waltham Forest, Redbridge and Tower Hamlets); SC1 (a life-sciences and creative-tech cluster in south London); and STRIDE (a programme to encourage innovation and enterprise, backed by the boroughs of Lambeth, Lewisham, Wandsworth and Southwark); and the Knowledge Quarter, undergoing a renaissance (led by Camden Council, with regeneration of King's Cross and Bloomsbury). Each competes for the best lifestyle offer for its residents, to retain and attract talent, and for the most visible and tangible manifestations of inclusive growth.

These clusters are already characterized by the juxtaposition of higher-education centres across the arts, science and technology with emerging start-ups and world-class international businesses, eager to be at the forefront of the very best, cutting-edge talent and innovation London has to offer. The formation of these purpose-built cross-sector clusters across the city will further enable councils to deliver a more impactful place for their residents and commercial tenants alike, as the fusion of education, enterprise and cultural innovation continues to drive the creation of wealth and inclusive growth for London's citizens.

The London of the future is not a utopia. The London of the future is a real place, with real challenges. But in true London fashion, the Londoners of the future will collaborate and co-design the solutions to the socio-economic and environmental challenges they face, building on this city's 2,000-year-old foundations, applying their own entrepreneurial, resourceful and creative DNA to every problem.

The London of the future will continue to transform challenges into opportunities for its citizens.

The London of the future will stay true to its roots: retaining and nurturing its eclectic communities as they continue to be the thread in London's tapestry as a truly regenerative city.

The London of the future will be resilient to global shocks, will outperform its international rivals in attracting foreign direct investment and will retain the talent it grows and nurtures because the London of the future will have recognized and embraced the reality that without cherishing our diverse culture, this city will not survive.

Notes

1 See www.un.org/development/desa/ disabilities/envision2030-goal11.html.
2 Simon Dixon, Ceri Smith and Anel Touchet, 'The Disability Perception Gap', policy report, May 2018.
3 Quoted in Laura Snoad, 'Design Can Is Out to Tackle the Design Industry's Lack of Representation', *It's Nice That*, 13 August 2019, www. itsnicethat.com/news/design-can-online-tool-representation-digital-120819.
4 Christina Mallon, 'The Disabled Community Is the World's Third-Largest Economic Power', Yahoo! Finance, 10 September 2019.

Giving Back to the City

Yvonne Farrell and Shelley McNamara,
Grafton Architects

A core challenge for architecture is always to see what it can give back to
the city. Whether architects are building for a private client, public body
or educational institution, they still have to deal with the cost of land and
making the most of a site. There are client needs on one side and planning
limits on the other, but no matter what the pressures are, at Grafton
Architects we're always trying to think about the overall generosity of
a building or landscape. This might involve creating a small garden or
something of beauty that the citizen can enjoy as they walk past, even if
they can't enter the space. We understand these concepts by looking at the
architecture of the past, which often has a kind of permanence that can
teach us how to build for the next one hundred years.

Empty or abandoned spaces make cities feel lifeless. People are the
essential component for the pleasure, safety and well-being of cities. The
question is how to make a city of welcome at a time when populations are
in transit. The role of architecture and of cities is to make places for people
– whether they're locals or immigrants: it's important that they feel a sense
of dignity, that they're respected and appreciated. Two of our buildings in
London – Town House for Kingston University and the Marshall Building
at the London School of Economics and Political Science (LSE) – both

respond to the needs of the institutions and their student populations, while addressing the city around them and creating a robust structure that will stand the test of time. We were inspired by some of the great spaces of London, such as the Royal Festival Hall and its undercroft along the South Bank: they create a landscape where people do all sorts of things beyond a prescriptive programme. The Town House is a twenty-four-hour building; its intensive use by students is the reason for a palpable sense of security there. Similarly, the ground floor of the Marshall Building has been designed for life to happen. Institutes are inherently space-hungry but a spirit of generosity makes a free space for people to enjoy.

Learning from the past

In 2022 the Sir John Soane Museum – the house and museum of this renowned British architect of two centuries ago – hosted an exhibition, *Neighbours in Space and Time*, which focused on shared themes between Soane's historic buildings and our contemporary work. The process of developing the exhibition content involved deep research into London's past. We found ourselves looking at a time when the quality of light and the urban environment were damaged by the pollution from the coal-burning and industries embedded within the city. We noticed that the public space of Lincoln's Inn Fields had remained throughout the centuries, and that the common open space is still held as a generous and public 'room' for the citizen and the stranger. We love Soane's ability to carve architectural space with light. Light is timeless. The exhibition referred to a 5,000-year-old burial chamber, Newgrange in County Meath, Ireland, which pre-dates Stonehenge and the pyramids of ancient Egypt. At the winter solstice, the chamber is illuminated by the rising sun, celebrating the changing of the seasons. This raises the question of how far humans have come over thousands of years and what the concept of permanence means.

Low-tech approach to the future

If we're thinking about building for a London in one hundred years, we have to imagine a form of architecture where it is possible to peel back layers of technology to reveal the essential elements. Foundations and structures will last much longer than the mechanical and electrical services that are added and will be replaced over time. We have to think

The Town House,
Kingston University
London (2019), by
Grafton Architects.

about buildings that have the longevity to survive in a world of limited resources. Considering the free gifts that nature gives us, we have a collective responsibility to share finite materials and energy across the planet and create a type of sustainability that goes beyond simply clipping on solar panels. Our UTEC (University of Engineering and Technology) Campus in Lima, Peru, for example, captures the breeze from the Pacific Ocean, while creating layers of shade to protect occupants from the close-to-the-equator sun. City dwellers will need to reconsider their lifestyles and means of travel, and find methods to reduce pollutants and increase biodiversity within the urban confines. We're more creatures of nature than we have been willing to admit over the last one hundred years, and this can inspire us.

Changing infrastructure

It's marvellous when infrastructure changes to become a public gift. An example is the transformation of the existing car park in front of the Town House. There were 150 car parking spaces along the busy roadway in front of Kingston University, which have been transformed into a linear park: good for the students and for local citizens. Canals that stretched across the United Kingdom, essentially the highways of the eighteenth century, are now becoming pleasant green routes for pedestrians and cyclists. We're seeing the harnessing of nature in London. Infrastructure can and will be transformed and synthesized for public benefit over time.

Creating a porous city

We were asked to give a lecture in the Marshall Building, in the Grand Hall on the ground floor, and we found ourselves surrounded by the sounds of the city thanks to the acoustic quality of the open space. Jazz was playing from the cafés in Lincoln's Inn Fields, while students moved in and out of

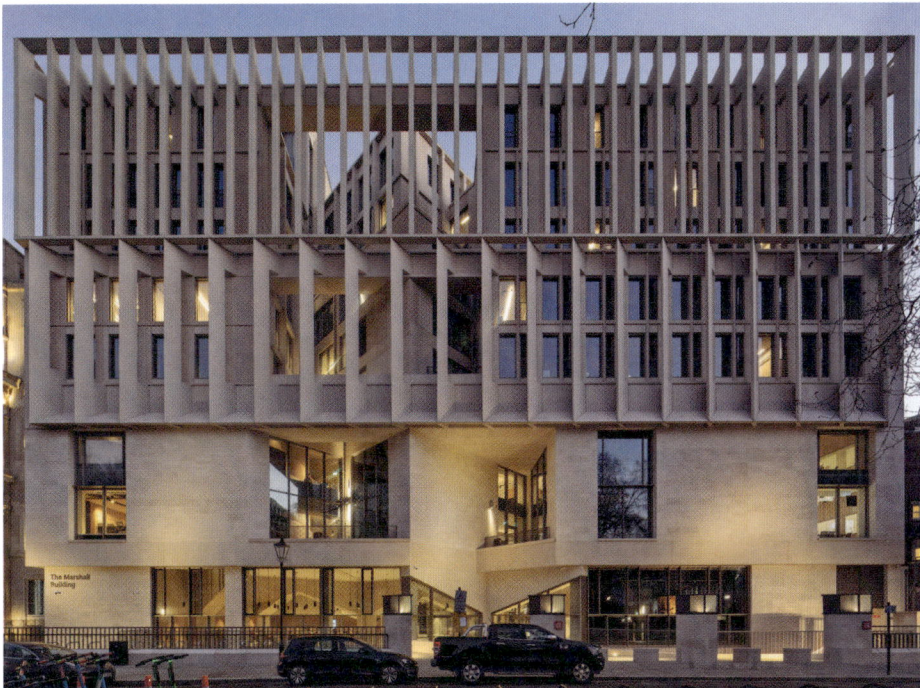

The Marshall Building, London School of Economics, Lincoln's Inn Fields (2022), by Grafton Architects.

the space as they wished because they felt it belongs to them. Some were wearing headphones and refused to move from their favourite seats in the Grand Hall, so everyone just had to make room (including an interested security guard who was keen to listen in). It was a wonderful experience because we weren't boxed into a room. It was more like giving a lecture out on the street or in a café. The porosity at LSE is a strength in itself. This is important for the future, as there is a real risk of fossilized thinking if we all go into our own closed rooms and don't hear the voices of others. As global temperatures rise, we will have to move towards a more open reality, allowing people and ideas to move freely. In the same way that we can't put up a wall around the edge of the Mediterranean or along the White Cliffs of Dover in Kent, equally we can't create intellectual walls. We talk about generosity through design. It's a philosophical and societal challenge to say that walls are about definition. The human spirit and human interaction are about a philosophical ability to accept otherness.

Locating yourself in the world

There is a floor in the Soane Museum that slopes towards the Thames, so there your relative gravity is both psychologically and physiologically orientated towards that great river. This reminds you that deep in your body, you are a creature of the earth. Architecture can help position us within our environments. Sadly, however, there's a belief that architects have lost the ability to make spaces where people come together. It is possible to claim space for the public through something as simple as installing a bench outside a town hall. Each building ripples and affects the space that surrounds it: it isn't all contained inside the front door when there's a place to be comfortable in the public realm. It's about everything from city-planning to small moments. For example, a cat might enjoy sitting in the warmth of the sunshine. That hasn't changed since pre-Egyptian times.

Learning from COVID-19

During the darkest days of the COVID-19 pandemic, when the cities were empty and silent and lonely, we realized that the city is a kind of a social machine based on daily interactions. We have to learn from those dreadful experiences and plan for fresh air and distance. Viruses will continue to roam the Earth in different ways. It's beholden on all civilizations to have spaces where, for example, school classrooms could be outside, and where people have access to generous terraces. Humans are actually much more versatile than we think. It's often important to change the mindset. We can learn by looking at the great cities, designed hundreds of years ago and still beautifully contributing to the quality of life.

Walking through the fifteenth-century Ospedale Maggiore in Milan, one of the oldest hospitals in Italy, you can see the investment in long-term building. The circulation is external and there are numerous beautiful staircases and gates but no doors; while outside you're moving in a protected microclimate. You're connected to the sky and to fresh air, which are vital in terms of health and well-being. We were fortunate enough to be standing in the forecourt of the historic Basilica of Sant'Ambrogio in Milan one day when the heavens opened and four gargoyles washed the pouring rain on to the courtyard floor, like a waterfall. The water then flowed through a cast-iron manhole in the middle of the courtyard. It was beautiful to hear and to feel the rain. We spend enormous amounts of time in the design of buildings trying to deal with all the things that go into their infrastructure, such as water attenuation. In reality, you just want to celebrate rain or capture wind: to work with nature, not try to conquer or tame it. There is a strong argument that sealed buildings are not healthy buildings. And instead of spending money on mechanical machinery to move air from one place to another, you could just make the volume twice the height and create that movement naturally, making a building that is comfortable.

Planning for the future

Humans should, as a global culture, ask that buildings demand less of resources and become ways of solving the particular issues of geography or climate. It would be amazing if we could all become more self-sufficient. There will always be buildings, such as hospitals, that require more energy, but in more ordinary places we could share the resources responsibly, rather than just being greedy. There will be technological innovations but each has an unexpected knock-on effect. For example, think about the impact that the car and the lift have made on cities and planning. We must have a value system that's generous to other human beings, both within our immediate circles and at a global level. We have to realize that we're sharing the Earth with eight billion neighbours and the challenges that this brings.

Learning from London's Peers
An Interview with Smith Mordak

Rob Fiehn

How do we mobilize cities to create any kind of political or cultural change, let alone the kind of transformational shift that is necessary for some sort of climate justice? There's a big discrepancy between what we need to do and the way things currently are. We can talk about the immediate headline requirements, such as retrofitting all our existing buildings or reducing the embodied carbon in construction, but perhaps we should also talk about what infrastructure is required to actually make it possible to reach climate targets. There is a role for governments to regulate and incentivize sustainable design – whether it's by quicker planning determination or by tax rebates – but by taking an infrastructural approach, they can enable system change at the scale needed.

In 2005 London signed up to the C40 Clean Construction Accelerator (a commitment to ensuring that buildings and infrastructure support a green agenda and promote healthy, sustainable, energy-efficient communities), which is already being implemented in such cities as Budapest, Los Angeles, Mexico City, Oslo and San Francisco. Over the last few years Smith Mordak and colleagues at the international consultancy Buro Happold have undertaken deep-dive studies into cities around the world, looking at ways in which they can use their local powers to

Extinction Rebellion march in central London, 12 October 2019.

transition to clean construction in a holistic way – including prioritizing reuse of existing buildings, optimizing structural designs, adopting bio-based materials and using different kinds of machinery. When cities sign up to the Accelerator, they commit to reducing their embodied carbon emissions by 50 per cent by 2030 for all new buildings and major infrastructure projects.

In some parts of the world the local municipality is able to play a larger role in determining the building codes and materials used in construction. The United Kingdom's cities are limited in the powers they have but are still able to make a difference within the built environment, for example through creating enabling infrastructure. 'To enable a truly circular built environment,' Smith Mordak explains, 'we need sorting and storage facilities where materials can be bought after demolition and used again, training so that everyone throughout the supply chain can understand how their own operations interface with the wider circular economy, and data-sharing platforms so that it's easy to list available materials and share them with a wide pool.' These sorts of ideas have the most impact when employed at a reasonable scale and cities are perfect for that. Perhaps in a massive city such as London, it's individual boroughs that can implement these large-scale solutions effectively.

If cities have the budgets and power to make these big infrastructural changes, the next opportunity is found at procurement. Taking a different approach to projects that are commissioned and funded at a metropolitan level can bring substantial wider benefits. Mordak gives an example from Exeter City Council: 'In 2009 they decided to build all their social housing to Passivhaus standards (the highest standards for reducing the energy consumption of buildings). This initially cost them around 20 per cent more than conventional methods, but as they kept up the requirement, year after year, the supply chains upskilled and invested, bringing the cost premium down to just 4 per cent for the council, and of course saving the residents of the homes substantial sums in energy bills.' This shows that public procurement can create positive knock-on effects that benefit the whole industry. 'Some might argue that we shouldn't be using the public purse in this way,' suggests Mordak, 'that private investment should be tasked with paying for the transition to better ways of working. But unless private investors are incentivized to create shared benefits, this isn't going to happen. We could try to create convoluted mechanisms to attract profit-seeking investment, and that may be part of the solution, but to me it also makes sense for shared infrastructural improvements to be funded through shared – i.e. public – funds.' Despite the prevailing wisdom, sustainability is not necessarily more expensive in terms of labour and materials in the medium to long term, but the transition may require investment to challenge established supply chains, which have been based historically on a race to the bottom. 'The public sector is perfectly positioned to normalize new ways of designing and constructing buildings and bring the commercial side of things along with it,' says Mordak.

There are many international examples that London could learn from to reach its environmental targets. In Milan the municipal authorities have the ability to track all the vacant and derelict spaces within the city. They have made a commitment to bring buildings back into use within eighteen months of their being added to this register. This is a good example of a platform that makes the most of basic information. In New York the city has created the Clean Construction Executive Order 23, which ensures that low-carbon concrete and steel, as well as low-carbon construction machinery, are used in all municipal projects. Oslo is using a procurement process in which the use of zero-emissions machinery gets awarded extra points. This has been in place for a while, and the municipality estimates that 15 per cent of sales of new construction machinery is electric equipment. From looking at various schemes around the world, it becomes clear that once public procurement starts requiring something, the industry gets the signal that it's worth aligning with these new norms, benefiting both public and private projects.

We've so far had twenty-seven iterations of the United Nations Climate Change Conference of the Parties (COP), but progress is happening slowly, if at all, because so many of the solutions being banked on are just that: looking to make money out of climate action. For Mordak, 'there's a fundamental problem with trying to profiteer our way to a habitable planet. If we're going to realize a global economy based on thriving ecosystems for humans and non-humans alike, we need that economy to be circular and redistributive, not extractive and not driving ever-deepening inequality.' Are too many of the current solutions aimed at incentivizing climate action with tax breaks or financial inducements that disproportionately benefit rich homeowners and large developers? Are we just further entrenching inequality at both national and international levels in different ways? What will it take to stand up to this trend? Will those who are worst affected come together and hold the global élite to account? Or will financial strength, physical resilience and emotional wisdom be eroded to such an extent by dispossessing systems that people will feel even less able to challenge their employers, landlords and government representatives?

'We need to support each other to maintain the financial, physical and emotional viability of collective action,' says Mordak. 'Because it's often in collective action that we find the seeds of a better future all around us, alive right now!' Collaboration at the scale of community groups often provides examples of mutual aid and energy where people are working together for a common purpose and creating that much-needed resilience. Within these groups we see how it is possible to share resources and burdens. There are lots of published precedents that showcase this kind of social justice but those conversations aren't breaking through to international organizations or big politics. How do we create space so that this kind of thinking can get a proper platform? 'Our approach with the C40 Clean Construction Deep Dives,' explains Mordak, 'was to explore ways in which we can mobilize the powers that cities already have for affecting change. If we can start approaching this by remobilizing existing infrastructure, things start to feel much more possible: imagine if a supermarket network was refocused away from environmental and financialextraction,and towards nature-based carbon sequestration and a shift to plant-based diets, or imagine if public services were unsiloed and reorganized around predistribution and preventative care. There's so much we could do under a different economic paradigm. This is the kind of conversation that we need to be having at COP28.'

Sadly, London doesn't have as much power as some cities to effect real change, but there's something to be said for boroughs and neighbourhoods if you want to explore a really potent scale for activity. The Buro Happold team worked on Hackney's *Climate Action Plan*, which shows what can be achieved at local level. While cities may not be able to reshape national economic policies, perhaps they can act as enablers so that different parts of the system can do what's needed to lay the foundations for broader change.

CLEAN CONSTRUCTION
MEXICO CITY
CITY KEY ACTIONS

With support from

C40 CITIES   BURO HAPPOLD   Oslo   IKEA

Benefits

- Support improvements in economic and labour productivity
- Encourage sustainable production and consumption practices
- Mitigation of risks to physical and mental health
- Foster inclusive, just and transparent governance
- Affordable, high-quality and accessible housing
- Sustainable management of public budgets
- Protection and enhancement of water quality
- Protection and enhancement of air quality
- Support the creation of green jobs and skills
- Reduced noise pollution

Climate action can take place at the household scale, neighbourhood scale, borough scale, city scale, national scale and international scale. Cutting across all these are different networks, corporations and ways of working. We need to understand how all those systems interact with one another and figure out how we can direct them towards the greater problem. For Mordak, central to effecting change at city scale is infrastructure: 'What I mean when I talk about infrastructure is the physical, digital and social means by which we organize and provision ourselves – how we look after each other. There's a lot of really valuable infrastructure within London, from the transport networks to the book club round the corner you've never heard of. There's a huge amount to do, but it's in this interconnected web of formal and (especially) informal infrastructure that I find hope that London can get this done.'

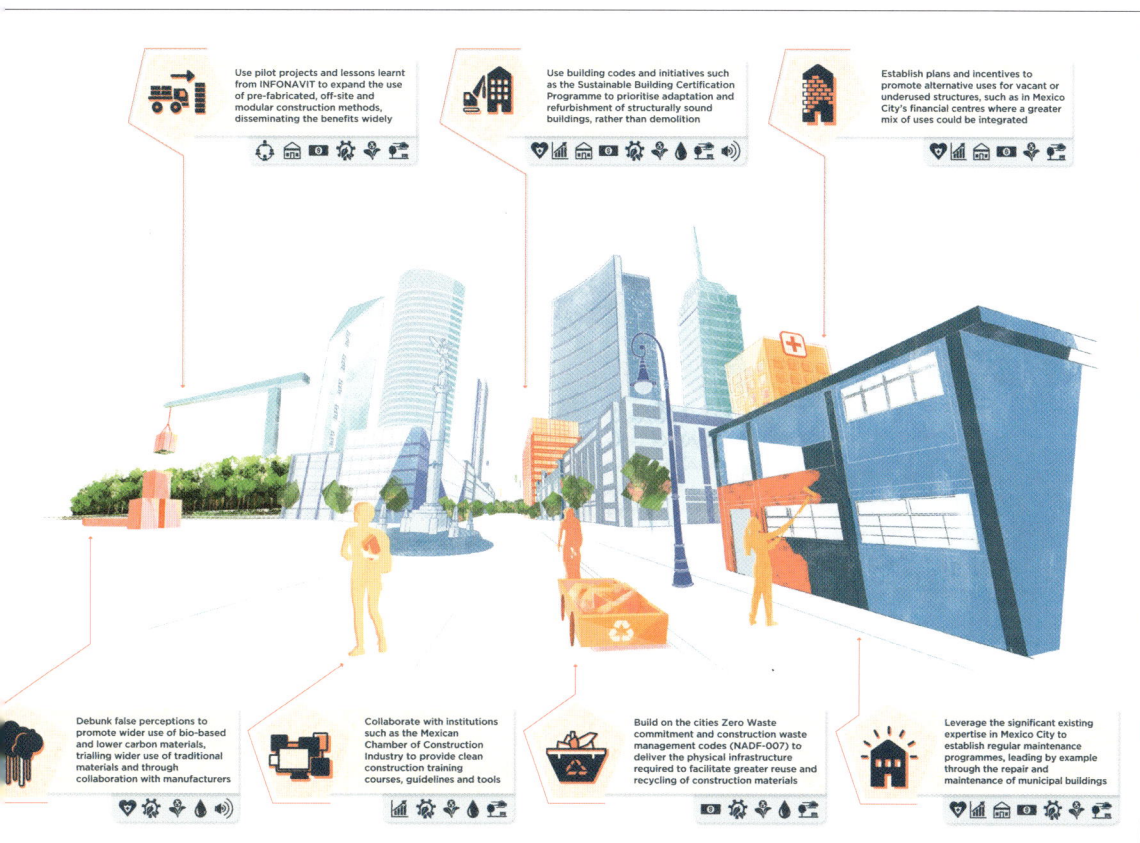

Clean Construction Mexico City by Buro Happold, a global investigation highlighting how clean construction could be achieved in different parts of the world, using local power and expertise.

Contributor Biographies

Roma Agrawal MBE is an engineer, author and broadcaster.

Claire Bennie is an architect and director of the housing development consultancy Municipal, which advises public landowners.

Mark Brearley is an architect and a professor of urbanism at London Metropolitan University. He is also proprietor of the long-established London tray and trolley manufacturer Kaymet, and since 2010 has been cataloguing manufacturers in the city.

Gillian Darley OBE is a widely published writer and architectural historian.

Yvonne Farrell and Shelley McNamara are founding partners of Grafton Architects, winners of the Pritzker Prize in 2020, the RIBA Stirling Prize and the Mies van der Rohe Prize in 2021 for the Townhouse building for Kingston University London.

Rob Fiehn is a London-based communications consultant specializing in architecture and design. He also takes on advisory roles, acting as chair for the Museum of Architecture, board member of the Blackhorse Workshop in Walthamstow, and trustee at The London Society.

Adam Nathaniel Furman is a British artist and designer of Argentine and Japanese heritage, who lives and works in London. They trained in architecture, and their atelier works in spatial design and art of all scales, from video and prints to large public artworks and architecturally integrated ornament, as well as products, furniture, interiors, publishing and academia.

Kat Hanna is an urbanist and built environment strategist who has spent the past decade working in the real-estate and London policy sectors.

Sarah Ichioka is an urbanist, curator, writer and founder of the strategic consultancy Desire Lines. She advocates for regenerative design and development in response to the planetary emergency.

Indy Johar MBE is an architect and co-founder of Dark Matter, a field laboratory that aims to redesign the urban institutional infrastructure in radical terms.

Yasmin Jones-Henry is a writer for the *Financial Times* and a cultural strategist who focuses on the intersections of fashion and finance, and culture and commerce.

The Victoria and Albert Museum East (2023) in Stratford by O'Donnell + Tuomey is a collaboration with the Smithsonian Institution in Washington.

Jude Kelly CBE is a theatre director, former artistic director of the Southbank Centre (Britain's largest cultural institution), and founder and CEO of the WOW Foundation, which creates festivals and events across six continents, reaching millions of women and girls.

Baroness Lawrence of Clarendon OBE is a campaigner who has promoted reforms of the police service. She was created a life peer in 2013.

Anna Minton is a writer and journalist, and Reader in Architecture at the University of East London. Her book *Big Capital: Who Is London For?* was published in 2017.

Smith Mordak is an award-winning architect, engineer and writer working across disciplines to realize a regenerative economy and built environment. They were appointed CEO of the UK Green Building Council in 2023.

Peter Murray is co-founder of New London Architecture, founder of the Festival of Architecture and chairman of the Temple Bar Trust. He was chair of The London Society 2014–21, rescuing it from certain closure.

Hugh Pearman MBE is an architectural writer, critic and consultant, and the author of *About Architecture: An Essential Guide in 55 Buildings* (2023).

Neal Shasore, an architectural historian, is head of school and chief executive officer at the London School of Architecture.

Carolyn Steel is a leading thinker on food and cities. She is the author of the award-winning *Hungry City: How Food Shapes Our Lives* (2008) and *Sitopia: How Food Can Save the World* (2020).

Mark Stevenson is a writer, businessman and reluctant futurologist.

Tony Travers is an academic and journalist who specializes in local government.

Leanne Tritton is chair of The London Society. She is the founder and managing director of ING Media, a communications agency focusing on contemporary architecture, design and the built environment.

Sponsors and Supporters

The London Society is grateful to the following people, companies and organizations, which helped to make the publication of this book possible.

Sponsors

BDP
Alan Baxter Foundation
Harriet's Trust
Fabrix

And our special thanks for the donation in memory of Derek and Sheila Melluish.

Gold Patrons

Toby Lloyd
John Nordon
Leanne Tritton

Patrons

Child Graddon Lewis
Hawkins\Brown
Jamie Ritblat

Supporters

David Ainsworth
Anthony Michal Aldous
Peter Allott-Fletcher
J. Barlow
Richard Barras
Terence Bendixson
Carlo Benigni
Rumi Bose
John Bowman
Gregory Bricusse
Anthony Briginshaw
Stuart Brooks
Don Brown
Alan Burns
Rosie Cade
Jessica Cargill Thompson
James Carter
Darryl Chen
N.A. Christodoulou
Sue Clark
Michael Cmar
Freya Cobbin
Barry Coidan
Laura Collins
James Collister
Dr Alina Congreve
Countryside Partnerships
Michael Coupe
Jeremy Cross
Katherine Darton
M.W. Davis
Clare Delmar
Emma Dent Coad
Alpa Depani
Alasdair Dixon
Sally Dore
Mark Driscoll
Andrew Duncan
David Edgar
Max Edwards
Zakia Elvang
Yusuf Erol
Julia Fiehn
Carole Fletcher
Mike Flood Page

Robin Forrest
Roger de Freitas
Adam Furman
Agapi Fylaktou
Neil Galway
Des Garrahan
Peter George
Arjan Geveke
Anna Gibb
Jana Gough
Kim Gray
Alison Griffin
David Hahn
Clarissa Hanna
Kat Hanna
Ruth Hazeldine
Sir Peter Hendy
Andrew Henriques
Adam Heppinstall
Dave Hill
Katherine Holman
Jack Hopkins
Ben Hume-Paton
Frank Jeffs
P.S. Jenkinson
Andrew Kelly
Frank Kelsall
Richard Keys
Stephen Kingsley
Paul Koopman
Guy Lambert
Eric Large
Barry Le Jeune
Alan Leibowitz
Edwin Lerner
William Linskey
London Communications
  Agency Ltd
Paul McAdam
Catherine McGuinness
Nicholas McKeogh
Janet McLeavy
David McRedmond
David Maddox
Igor Marko
Peter Martin

Simon Martin
Janet Elizabeth Mellor
Jonathan Milward
Semakaleng Moema
Laura Morgan
Charlotte Morphet
Julia Moseley
Caroline Mulhall
Laura Murray
Peter Murray
Elis Mutlu
Jeremy H.M. Newsum
Fabienne Nicholas
Chris Paddock
Simon Pitkeathley
Ian Pleace
Clive H. Price
Jack Pringle
Eleanor Purser
Chris Remo
Christopher Rhodes
Paul Rhodes
John Rowe
Alex Sarll
Martin Scholar
Zoe Sellers
Anthony Shapland
Jeremy Simons
Russell Southwood
Visakha Sri Chandrasekera
Ellie Stathaki
Paul Steeples
Ian Swankie
Dave Taylor
Andrew Templeton
Mark Thomlinson
Geoffrey Thurley
Carole Tyrrell
Ed Watson
Nicholas Wells
Rosamund West
Dr Werner Wiethege
David Wilcox
Melissa Woolford
Sharon Wright
Anthony Zeilinger

Acknowledgements

London of the Future would not have been possible without the expertise and energy of The London Society trustee Rob Fiehn, who led the project through all aspects of development.

Special thanks to:

The London Society project working group

Leanne Tritton (Chair)
Don Brown (Director)
Alpa Depani
Barry Coidan
Nick McKeogh

The London Society Trustees

Mark Prizeman
Lucy Smith
Eric Sorensen
Yusuf Erol
Dave Hill
Kat Hanna
Diane Cunningham
Clare Delmar
Rowena Ellims (Programme
    Manager)

The London Society is also grateful to Hugh Merrell of Merrell Publishers, and to Nicola Bailey, Rosanna Fairhead and Nick Wheldon; to all those who provided illustrations for the book, especially Chris Hopkinson, Paul Raftery, Agnese Sanvito and Will Scott; to Adam Nathaniel Furman for the cover artwork; and to all the contributors.

The publisher is grateful to Henry Russell and Chris Hopkinson for their contribution to the making of this book.

Picture Credits

Index

First published 2023 by
Merrell Publishers Limited, London
and New York

Merrell Publishers Limited
70 Cowcross Street
London EC1M 6EJ

merrellpublishers.com

British Library Cataloguing-in-Publication
    data:
A catalogue record for this book is
available from the British Library.

ISBN 978-1-8589-4710-5

Produced by Merrell Publishers Limited
Designed by Nicola Bailey
Project-managed by Rosanna Fairhead
Copy-edited by Sarah Yates
Proofread by Patricia Burgess
Indexed by Hilary Bird

Printed and bound in China

COVER IMAGE AND FRONTISPIECE:

Adam Nathaniel Furman
Sodom & Londinium
2023

Big, complex, degenerate, diverse and
wild, London is and has always been a
hotbed for brilliant deviance of all kinds,
as well as radical and inclusive politics.
This drawing dreams about a future
in which all its most wonderful and
contentious attributes dominate, and
are embodied in its architecture, which –
rather than being driven by commercial
exigencies – is driven by communities
and subcultures who have taken control
of the city's destiny through a speculative
new form of super-devolution.